DAVE LIEBER'S
WATCHDOG
NATION
Bite Back When Businesses
and Scammers Do You Wrong
W
WINNER OF TWO NATIONAL BOOK AWARDS FOR SOCIAL CHANGE

ALSO BY DAVE LIEBER

Shop at www.YankeeCowboy.com/store

The Dog of My Nightmares: Stories by Texas Colunnist Dave Lieber

Bad Dad
A True Texas Crime Thriller

The High-Impact Writer:
Ideas, Tips & Strategies to Turn Your Writing World Upside Down

I Knew Rufe Snow Before He Was a Road
(with Tim Bedison)

Give Us a Big Hug
(with Tim Bedison)

DAVE LIEBER'S WATCHDOG NATION®

Bite Back When Businesses and Scammers Do You Wrong

By Dave Lieber

Published in cooperation with the *Fort Worth Star-Telegram*

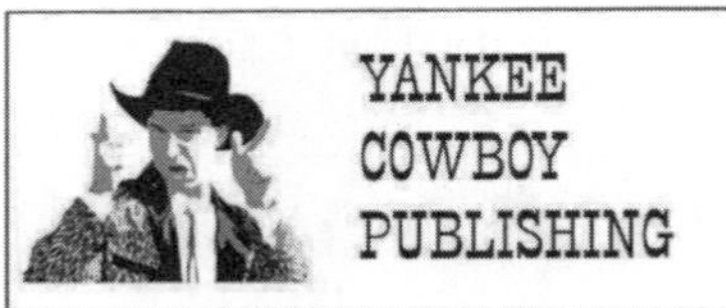

Published by Yankee Cowboy Publishing
Watchdog Nation® is a registered trademark.

FIRST EDITION, October 2008
SECOND EDITION, (Revised & Expanded) January 2010
THIRD EDITION, January 2012

Yankee Cowboy Publishing
P.O. Box 123
Keller, Texas 76244-0123

For information on Yankee Cowboy Publishing,
contact publisher@yankeecowboy.com or write to the above address.
Phone: 1-800-557-8166

Book Site: www.WatchdogNation.com
Author sites: www.YankeeCowboy.com
www.DaveLieber.org
Twitter @DaveLieber

ISBN 978-0-9708530-2-8

Library of Congress Number: 2009939093

PRINTED IN CANADA

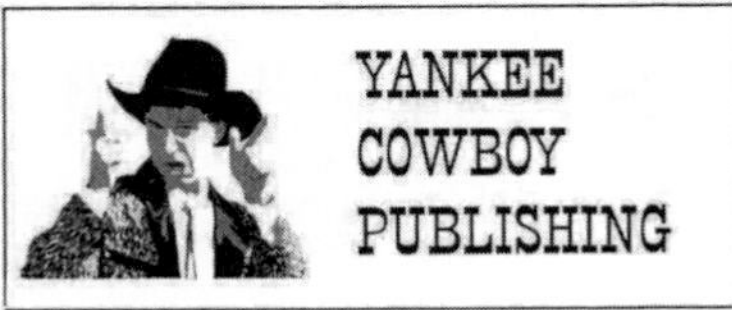

This book is dedicated to

DETECTIVE DOMINIC LAROCCA
You were always there when I needed you

&

LOIS NORDER
Editor, mentor and friend

W
WATCHDOG NATION

The Watchdog Nation®
Manifesto

We, the members of The Watchdog Nation, do everything in our power to defend ourselves and help others when businesses and scammers do us wrong.

We combat unfairness and unethical behavior by using every resource at our command in a fair and ethical way to prove that, in the end, the good guys win. (Especially if there are enough of us!)

"Truth, justice and the American way" is no comic-book cliché to us. In The Watchdog Nation, it is the standard by which everyone is held accountable.

Dave Lieber

LEADER OF THE WATCHDOG NATION

The goal of Watchdog Nation® is for you to spread these ideas and strategies with others.

As American writer and historian Henry B. Adams once wrote, "A teacher affects eternity; he can never tell where his influence stops."

Go affect humanity.

Watchdog Nation® Awards

2009 Winner of two top awards from the National Society of Newspaper Columnists. "Every city needs a Dave Lieber," one judge said. "Dave Lieber's columns quickly and easily create a sense of outrage in a reader. He writes about rip-offs, scams and jerks who take advantage of the most vulnerable people in society."

2009 Winner of Defending the Disadvantaged/First Amendment Award from the Society of Professional Journalists.

2009 Winner of the Next Generation Indie Book Award for Social Change.

2009 Winner of the National Best Books Award for Social Change, sponsored by USA Book News.

Judges in the 2009 Benjamin Franklin Awards call *Dave Lieber's Watchdog Nation* "A really useful book! ... I just kept flipping from page to page, case to case; laughing and learning from the lead watchdog." A second judge: "I loved this book! It addresses in a very clear fashion how to stop scammers, as well as how to resolve bill disputes with AT&T, the electric company, etc. … Highly recommended."

Preface

One month before the first edition of this book was released, our nation suffered a catastrophic financial collapse that became known as the Great Recession. The book could not have been timelier.

For decades, the so-called experts and government leaders promised us that the "fundamentals" of the U.S. economy were sound. They promised us they were taking care of us, that everything would be all right.

We know better now.

Americans everywhere began to understand the great lesson of this era: The only one who can protect you, your family and your business is YOU! You must be your own watchdog in all matters of your life.

At my newspaper job, I get more mail than anyone. Each letter is a complaint about a company or individual that the letter writer does business with. Each contains a sad story of betrayal and loss. It breaks my heart that because of time constraints I can't help everyone.

This book is designed to show you how to help yourself.

Just like you, I was brought up to believe the world was a good place. But now we understand that institutions such as our banks, credit card companies, utilities, service repair industries, you name it, often don't have our best interests at heart. Sometimes their behavior toward us is nothing short of criminal.

For every Bernard Madoff and R. Allen Stanford who allegedly swindle big, there are thousands of others who try to scam us in small ways.

In the year that has passed since Watchdog Nation® and its sister Web site WatchdogNation.com were introduced to the world, I was a near-victim of eight attempted scams. (Yes, I keep count because for me, these are learning opportunities.)

Let me share:

1. Someone walked into a Wal-Mart and wrote a fraudulent $279 check. The check contained my correct name and address, but it wasn't mine. I learned about this when a debt collection agency called seeking payment.
2. While researching a software purchase, a salesman assured me that customer service would assist me with any installation problems. When I tried to install and ran into a problem, customer service tried to charge me $79.
3. I revisited a company's Internet site where years before I purchased a check endorsement stamp. The company took the money but didn't send me the stamp.
4. Another Internet retailer took my money for a promotional item I bought for Watchdog Nation and tried to avoid delivery.
5. A bank notified me that my financial records were stolen – known as a data breach. Unknown people could gain access to my financial information.
6. Five years of my credit history vanished from my credit report. This meant I could not successfully apply for any credit cards until my history was restored.
7. Someone tried to use my publishing company's post office box to apply for a credit card.
8. A neighbor knocked on my door to explain that she had switched electric companies. After offering my condolences (I pay a lower rate at my electric company), she explained that her new company had transposed our addresses and instead was switching me. I had to call and cancel. If I hadn't been told, my electric bill would have jumped 30 percent.

If these mishaps happen to me, I know they happen to you.

Let's enter the world of Watchdog Nation and learn how to overcome this.

This book is for the Jeffs of the world

Jeff snapped. That's not like him. He works in social services and has compassion for people. He understands that people make mistakes, and he believes in a second chance, even a third.

But every so often, something gets his dander up.

This time, it was a $4 mistake.

"The amount is irrelevant," Jeff says. "It will barely buy you a gallon of gas."

But then he says something that I hear time and again about companies that owe their customers small amounts of money: It's not the money; it's the principle.

"The problem is that nobody is willing to take responsibility for the problem and apologize for the error," Jeff says.

It all started when Jeff was charged $90 for work done on his car. But as he stood before the cashier, he saw that the invoice was totaled incorrectly. He was being overcharged by $4.

He asked the cashier. She fetched the manager. The manager assured him the total was correct.

So he paid the bill and left the store. But the overcharge hung over him like a dark cloud.

A few days later, he went back to the store and asked that the bill be corrected.

He was rebuffed again.

At some point, desire can become obsession, and that's what happened here.

He went back a third time to ask for his $4. He got the same answer.

Most people would give up. Not Jeff, apparently a true member of The Watchdog Nation®.

On the fourth visit, he recalled, "I took a printout with my own math to show them in black and white that the amount was wrong."

OK! Uncle! The manager had had enough of this guy. He handed Jeff four bucks, probably expecting the matter to go away forever.

He didn't know jack, er, Jeff.

Jeff sent a letter of complaint by certified mail to the business' supervisor and another to the local owner. He told them what happened.

Neither bothered to reply.

So he took it up the next notch: He wrote to the corporation whose name is on the front door of the auto dealership. His reply? A voice-mail message from a woman at headquarters telling him to expect a call from the business' supervisor.

He waited. And waited. A week passed. Nobody called. He called the woman back at the automaker's headquarters. Sorry, she said. Nothing more she could do.

Jeff stepped up still another rung on the company ladder. He contacted the supervisor of the woman at headquarters and reported that his complaint had been ignored. The supervisor repeated the company line: *Sorry. See ya.*

Had Jeff run out of rungs? Not exactly. He could have sent letters to each member of the company's board of directors. Or he could do what he did: Contact me. Sometimes just talking about these common business dysfunctions is therapy in The Watchdog Nation.

"I think my experience is highly representative of everything that's wrong with the American way of doing business today," he says. "The employees didn't care about doing their job properly because they knew their supervisor wasn't going to hold them accountable. And the owner didn't care because he knew, quite correctly, that while the corporate bosses might make a small show of it, ultimately they weren't going to hold him accountable either."

Of all the contacts Jeff made, nobody accepted responsibility.

"I guess that was too much to expect," he says.

Now he is torn. He loves the automobile involved. But he will never buy from the carmaker again.

The company stands to lose a loyal customer over $4 and an apology.

A few years ago, I would have thought that Jeff was being a bit obsessive. But now, after hearing hundreds of stories like his, most involving more than $4, I don't trivialize the experience.

Get this: Jeff is not the one with the problem.

If the Jeffs of the world lose their passion to fight for things no matter how big or small, then who is left among us who will fight at all?

This book is for Jeff—and for you.

Let's fight back.

FROM THE DESK OF DAVE LIEBER

Jessica: *Would you like to try this with the first 30 days for free under the terms I've just described?*

Dave Lieber: *Is there any other catch? Please let me know. I should warn you that I have been known to complain quick and loud if something is hidden from me. I am the leader of The Watchdog Nation—a consumer advocate by avocation. This is what I do for a living. So no other catches?*

Jessica: *There is no catch, just great savings as a thank you to valued Howard Johnson customers.*

— Dave Lieber in an online chat with saleswoman "Jessica" of Travelers Advantage Club. March 25, 2008

Note to self:
If I have problem canceling that stupid travel club membership, mention it in the book.

Introduction

Every day, I spend about 15 minutes on the phone or on the computer trying to correct a problem that has to do with one of the companies with which I do business.

In the old days, it took one phone call. These days, it's never solved in one phone call, and the people I talk to are rarely local. They work off a script. Today's customer service representatives have no record of my call from the day before. Or so they say. So I have to start all over again.

Why does it have to be this way?

It doesn't.

OK, I'm cranky. Today my 15 minutes were spent trying to cancel a travel club membership that promised to save me $30 on a motel room bill. The deal was I could get the $30 coupon and then cancel without a hassle. But they "forgot" to send the coupon. It took three phone calls over a two-week period to cancel.

A travel club? Don't laugh. I never go for that stuff. But the original saleswoman popped up with such a beguiling sales pitch that I couldn't resist.

She literally popped into my life inside a chat box that burst forth on my computer screen while I was online making the motel reservation. Her question? *Do you want to save $30 on this bill?*

We chatted. She explained the deal. I grilled her like she was the star witness on the Senate Watergate committee. I even copied and saved the transcript of her pitch and my interrogation.

But as is always the case, after I agreed to the deal, there were the inevitable complications.

Fortunately, I taped all three of my follow-up phone calls to them. (In Texas, where I live, that's legal.)

On the third call, when the saleswoman tried to keep me from canceling by dangling club goodies in front of me, I said joyfully and confidently: "Ma'am, I have a transcript of the initial sales conversation. I have three tapes of my phone calls including this call. I also have the address of the attorney general in your home state. I am here right now to cancel and end this matter. Are you with me or not?"

She was with me.

Welcome, my friend, to The Watchdog Nation.

In The Watchdog Nation, we figure that if we are going to spend 15 minutes a day—two hours a week or four days a year—dealing with corporate goons and scammers, they are going to be 15 *quality* minutes. We are going to know what we are doing. We are out for the kill.

When I'm on hold, I'm plotting. When my call is lost overseas during a transfer from one department to another, I can't run fast enough to fill out a nasty customer survey to log my complaint. When I finally do get a human being who gives me a fake name ("Hi, my name is Biff"), I ask Biff for his full name, employee ID number and location of his office. They hate that.

Somebody will one day write a great book about bizarre customer service stories. This is not that book, although there are some bizarre stories in here. No, this book shows you how you can avoid being the star of one of those stories. This is a book with tips, tools and strategies that are designed to save time and energy and help you beat the system before it beats you.

You won't win every time. But you'll win more than you lose. And every time you get a refund and an apology, you strike a winning blow for The Watchdog Nation®.

But The Watchdog Nation is more than about solving your problems. It's about waking up the masses and alerting everyone to what many of us already suspect: We are in the midst of The Great Era of Scams. There's little difference, I think, between the phone company that tacks an extra charge on your bill and the guy on the street corner with a fold-up table asking you to guess which shell the bean is under.

There's always somebody looking to pick your pocket. When you complain, you find nobody willing to take ownership of a problem, barely any accountability and lots of promises made and then broken.

The Watchdog Nation seeks to inspire millions of Americans to rise up and bite back.

The Watchdog Nation is founded on a few simple ideas.

Until a few years ago, it was almost impossible to put the pieces of the puzzle together about the reputation and credibility of any business or individual. Today, with the click of a computer mouse, you can do an instantaneous background check and strike the mother lode.

But if it's too late for that, and you do fall prey to a scam or unfair business practice, it's now easier than ever to find out what laws or rules apply to you as the victim and to the scammer as the perpetrator.

By typing in key words in any search engine, you can locate laws, rules and regulations that apply to most situations in city, county, state and federal governments.

Most people don't know their rights. We have many. And now, it's easier than ever to learn what they are.

As part of this, these various government agencies have enforcement agents, inspectors and others who are supposed to monitor, accredit, certify or approve the activities of those engaged in various businesses. Often, though, because of negligence on the part of the government and an apathetic public, these enforcement staffs are cut to the bone. That's why The Watchdog Nation seeks, as a long-term goal, to beef up regulatory agencies, prosecutors and others that seek to protect the rights of consumers, the infirm, the disabled and the elderly. What good are laws against fraud, negligence and deceptive trade practices if you don't enforce them?

I have worked as a newspaperman for more than 30 years, half of that time with the *Fort Worth Star-Telegram*. There, as one of a handful of investigative columnists in the U.S., I learned how a few people can make a very big difference when it comes to bettering our lives.

Each week in my role as The Watchdog columnist, I hear from dozens of people who are at their wit's end in dealing with situations that reek of unfairness and sometimes criminality.

They want to fix their problem, but they don't know how. And they want to help others avoid the same mess.

In these pages, we'll share tales of struggle and triumph that will inspire you to fight back.

We need to stand up for ourselves because no one else is going to do it for us.

We are The Watchdog Nation.

TIP: Check 'em out...

Let's start with the single most important tip this book has to offer. (I know—dessert before the main meal.)

Today, scams are more prevalent than at any time in world history. It's easy to screw people, and hard to get caught. Too many scammers and too few investigators and prosecutors.

So you really have to protect yourself.

Here's the good news: It's easier to protect yourself than ever before. And it doesn't take much.

All you need to do is run a company's name through your favorite Internet search engine. (In addition to Google, use Bing.com, Viewzi.com, Dogpile.com and Icerocket.com, which may pick up different Web pages.)

If you want to hire Company XYZ, search like this:

"Company XYZ and scam"

"Company XYZ and rip-off"

If you don't have a computer, ask your librarian to do it for you.

If you get more than a few hits, there's a problem.

Watchdog Nation Core Principle #1:

Always search before you make the decision, not after

I call it The Watchdog Nation Test.

Before you buy anything or hire anyone, you must get into the habit of conducting a quick search on the Internet. Most people who get hurt do their searches afterward, but by then it's too late.

Still, for some, smart searching is difficult. I take it for granted that everyone knows how to search like me. But I've been doing computer searches for more than three decades.

I'll never forget the power I felt at my first newspaper job in the late 1970s when I could go to the "clips library" and look up any person or subject and instantly learn important details. By the 1980s these searches were done on computer databases. What instant knowledge and power!

I got in trouble once when I looked up a new girlfriend's family history and, on a date, started reciting the details of her father's car dealership business. She became upset, and I quickly learned that because you know something doesn't mean you have to talk about it.

Still, as recently as 15 years ago, much public information was still unavailable to me, even as a journalist. For example, if I wanted to trace an automobile license plate, I had to beg a police source. I'd get a lecture about how much trouble the officer could get in, and then he'd look up the name and address.

Now those databases are available, as are many other records for as little as $25 a year on a site such as www.PublicData.com.

Here are some basic search rules I follow.

1. Don't assume your first search on Google will lead to the correct answer. Some of the latest information on your search subject will not necessarily

pop up on Google's main page but could be found in blogs. Go to Google's "More" tab and click on "Blogs" to search. Or use another blog search engine to delve deeper.

2. Use quote marks to narrow results. For example, if you type in a product and you get a gazillion results, try it again with quote marks around the product's exact name and model number.
3. When you receive a letter, e-mail, phone call or fax that appears suspicious, put the contact phone number or the company name used in the sales pitch into a search box and see what pops up. Then try it again with the words scam, fraud and rip-off next to it. Within seconds, you may find others who have received the same bogus offer and did your research for you.
4. Don't believe everything you read on your screen. Somebody might post that something is a scam, even when it isn't. So keep reading. Dig a little deeper and come to your own conclusions.
5. You don't have to be a Twitter user to search Twitter. This real-time search engine might also help you find information about others who have the same problem. Go to this Web site—search.twitter.com—and type in a keyword about your problem.
6. If you want to keep tabs on a particular problem and learn more information as it becomes available, set up a Google News Alert, which will alert you when a particular phrase of your choosing pops up on the Internet. Do a search for "setup Google News Alert" to learn how to do it. For Twitter, use Tweetbeep.com to set up Twitter alerts that work the same way.
7. When you want to learn how to do something, don't forget to visit YouTube.com. Often, instructional videos will pop up with a lesson that shows you how.

When they come knocking, you go tappin'

Doug Black pulled out his checkbook.

The two college-age women standing on his front porch were close to making a sale. They told him they were college freshmen working on a communications class project. They wanted him to buy books and donate them to sick children at a local hospital. They said they lived nearby.

Black prepared to write a check for $54. But then, bam, just like that, he remembered that his computer was running in his home office just inside the door.

He asked the two women if their company had a Web site. They smiled and gave him the Web address.

"Give me a moment, OK?"

While the women waited outside, Black walked inside and sat at his laptop. He found the company's Web site. It looked reputable: "We are proud to bring the finest books and magazines to your door."

But Black, who works in his county courthouse's information technology department, didn't stop there. He placed the company name—Integrity Program—into a search engine, and the rest of the hits weren't so uplifting:

"If these people come to your door, do not buy anything from them. Do not let them into your home."

"Horror stories," stated another posting.

Black was smart shopping, 21st-century style.

Toting hand-held devices while we shop, we can check competitor prices and search for complaints on a product while standing in a store. We can learn if a salesman has a criminal record. If a doctor has been sued for malpractice.

Black's tappety-tap on the keyboard while talking to his visitors shows that it's getting harder to disguise who you are and what you do—as long as the customer is willing to do a little research first.

The real estate agent is showing you the neighborhood, and you are checking crime statistics.

The restaurant looks good, but what's the latest health inspection score?

As Black Googled the women outside his door, he asked about their communications class.

One mentioned her professor's name. Within seconds, Black had looked but couldn't find the name on the department's Web site.

"I'm just a freshman and don't pay attention to that stuff," the woman said.

Black walked back outside. He didn't tell the young women that within minutes he had learned enough to know he didn't want to do business with them. He put his checkbook away.

All he said was: "I couldn't find your professor's name on the Web site. Sorry then. I can't order unless you verify the information. If you can bring me back proof, I will order those books. Come back Friday or Saturday."

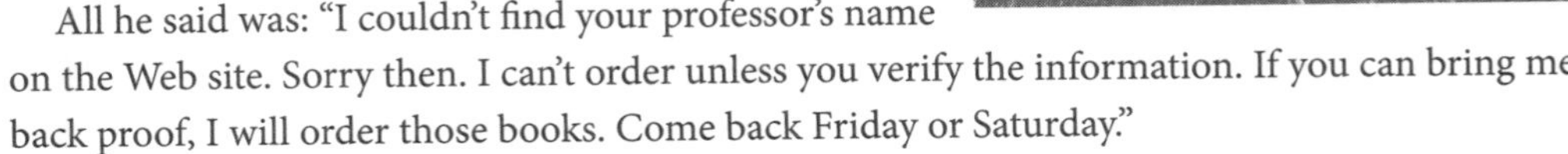

They said they would come back. But they never showed.

The man with the information knew too much about them.

Don't let salespeople inside your home. ■ Don't feel pressured to buy a product or service. ■ If you feel threatened or are made to feel guilty, that's the sign of a scam. Call the police. ■ Ask for identification and a company name, address and phone number. Make sure the seller can show the physical address, not a post office box. ■ Investigate them!

Yo, AT&T! What's your phone number?

Steve Hollern called to complain that he was having difficulty getting somebody from a certain large corporation on the telephone to help solve his problem.

He called a lot of different phone numbers, but could never reach the right one. When he called customer service, he talked to a company representative on the other side of the globe who couldn't help him.

He explained his frustration to me with a phrase that is becoming the mantra for frustrated American customers.

"I got tired of going round and round and round."

It was so frustrating that he finally gave up and wrote a letter to the company.

So I tried to help Hollern. But I ran into the same problem.

I couldn't find a phone number for the part of the company that I needed to talk with—the media relations department. These are the people who answer questions from pesky watchdog columnists like me.

I spent a half hour using all the resources at my fingertips—the Internet, directory assistance, even calling people in the company and asking them for the phone number. But I could never find the right number.

What company is this?

Why, it's the telephone company.

Hello, AT&T? Can you hear me now?

When I finally found a spokeswoman (by e-mail), she told me, "Most folks who go online prefer to reach us via e-mail."

Remember, this is the phone company speaking.

I asked why she didn't put a phone number for her office in the public domain like most other companies do. She never answered.

Could it be, I wondered, because people like Steve Hollern, frustrated beyond belief, might find it and call?

"I can't speculate on that," she answered.

I can. Complaints to AT&T are so voluminous that the company has to shield itself from its own customers.

AT&T wants you to call its toll-free customer service numbers found on your bill or on its Web site, but oftentimes, that's not going to get you a solution.

People complain to me all the time about how they have called the phone company time and again, but their problems are never solved.

That's why, sometimes, you need to find someone higher up in the food chain to help you.

And that's why AT&T shields its main office numbers and executives' direct lines from the rest of us.

The phone company doesn't want you to call.

So how do we beat that?

TIP: Go to this Web site: Zoominfo.com

Type in the name of the company you want to research. The main corporate number will come up. Sometimes, the names of the top executives will come up. Call and ask to be connected. If that doesn't work, search for some of their various organizations and associations. Keep researching. Somewhere, somehow, you will find a direct phone number or an e-mail address for them. Call or write. Briefly state your case. Seek pity. Ask for an "executive intervention."

AT&T's slogan: "Your world. Delivered." Yeah, right.

OK, since this is my book, I can write about what I want. And since the phone company bugs me to no end, I want to continue my rant.

The AT&T slogan used to be: "Your world. Delivered."

But what if you can't get a telephone book delivered?

Turns out that this problem is pretty common. One more example of the reduced customer service standards found almost everywhere.

Jean Neyland complained to me that she tried for months to get a White Pages phone book. She said she called AT&T for three months to ask but was always told to call again the next month.

I called the phone company for her. The next day, a book was delivered to her home.

"I had immediate service, thanks to you," she told me. "It's awfully hard to ask them questions when you are talking to a tape. This is as good as Christmas to me. You must have a magic wand."

No magic wand. I just had the correct phone number, which in the world of AT&T is a sort of magic all its own. They really don't want to hear from you.

Oh, if all the problems with them were as easy to solve as getting that phone book.

Richard Ellis said he had been stuck in an endless loop of AT&T's (supposed) customer service since October. Here's what happened.

His 82-year-old mother was getting bills for a phone number that resembled hers but had a different area code. Ellis said AT&T's response followed an annoying pattern.

He called the billing department, and a billing representative said it was a fraud problem. Transferred to the fraud department, Ellis was asked to re-explain his problem, which he did, before he was transferred back to billing. Back where he started, he was connected to a different person, who asked him to state his problem again.

Then he would speak to a supervisor, explain the problem again, and the supervisor would promise to fix it.

The next month another incorrect bill arrived, and Ellis would go through the loop again: billing, transferred to fraud, back to billing and then to a supervisor.

"It's just over and over and over," he told me.

"Finally in January, talking to the billing manager, I said, 'Look, I've explained this four months in a row. What I really would like is your name and number so when this comes up again, I can call you and talk to you so I don't have to explain this.'

"Well, this lady says, 'We don't give our name and number.' "

After Ellis refused to pay for the mistake, AT&T referred the bill to a credit agency, which began calling Ellis' mother for payment. Furious, Ellis called AT&T yet again and a representative told him to call the credit agency.

"You created the problem," he insisted. "And now you're telling me that AT&T can't fix it, and I have to go to a credit agency?"

"Let me transfer you somewhere else," he was told.

The next AT&T person he spoke with asked, "What are you calling me about?"

Ellis said, "Never mind."

Eventually, Ellis called me. I intervened.

I told AT&T that I would write about the story in my newspaper column.

AT&T fixed the problem.

I wrote about it anyway.

Dear AT&T, I've had enough...

Things got so bad that I decided to write an Open Letter to AT&T:

Dear AT&T,

I have a question for you: Why do so many people complain to me about your customer service? Repeatedly, they tell me about customer service reps that drop the ball about your U-verse television service.

See, I have this job that allows me to monitor in an unscientific way which companies are on top of their game. When I keep hearing from readers about one particular company, I know things aren't right.

Lately, I'm hearing about you.

When you rolled out your U-verse television service, were you prepared to handle your new customers and all the troubles they've had?

You do have a call center dedicated to U-verse troubleshooting, and your promised two-hour installation window for a technician visit is commendable—when it works.

Granted, J.D. Power and Associates named you the best TV provider in customer satisfaction for the region where I live. So good for you. But the folks who contacted Watchdog Nation apparently didn't vote.

I'm talking about customers like Shaun and Kim Hamblin, who ordered U-verse but waited three times for installers who never showed. And when one finally arrived, he accidentally cut their DSL line and they lost Internet service for days.

There's Cheryl Vieau, fighting a $225 disconnect fee for weeks without much success. "I have been on the phone, mostly on hold, for hours," she said.

Thomas Parker, fretting for a year about U-verse, said he is giving up: "I have no more patience for this. I haven't complained in over a month because what's the point?"

James Burke said six technicians visited his home, but none could fix his poor TV service. "No one seems to care about my problem," he said.

Seth Viertel has tried for months—"I am at my wits' end"—to get payments restored to his checking account that were originally credited to the wrong customer account. "AT&T's customer service is anything but," he said.

Rebates and rewards? Another sticky wicket. Charles Dempsey couldn't get his promised $50 gift card from you for signing up for your long-distance plan. Donald Martin is waiting for his referral reward, too. Someone on your end punched in a wrong number. "It seems there are so many little things that can disqualify one for a reward, and AT&T doesn't even let you know if they are not going to honor them," he said.

Complaints about your land-line and cellular service are rarer, but hey, you're the phone company. That's what you did for a century before you suddenly spread your wings into TV and computers.

Before you celebrate, though, I'd better mention Morgan Bilbo. He's still ticked at you because he continues to receive bills for calls he says he didn't make. "I am very upset and losing sleep over it," he said.

AT&T, maybe I'm being too rough, but maybe not. Listen to Joyce Polson, who began her letter to me about her U-verse/Internet package this way: "The worst day of my life was the day my husband switched us to this messed-up service."

All these customers contacted me because they couldn't get anywhere with you. I passed them on to your spokeswoman, and she took over from there.

But AT&T, I really don't want to be your middleman.

Get it together, please,

Dave

Watchdog Nation Core Principle #2:

Make the company person on the phone line accountable to you

When you call the phone company, bank, credit card company or whomever, you often speak to people on the other side of the world who hold 90 percent of the power. You don't know who they are. And you beg them for your money back.

Here's how a citizen of Watchdog Nation changes a 90-10 power balance to 50-50 or even one in your favor.

Rep: OK, thank you for verifying your information. How can I make your day at Bank of USA happy in every way?

Me: Before I tell you my problem, let me ask you a few questions. What's your name?

Rep: I don't have to tell you because you'll get a reference number at the end.

Me: Well, great, but I don't talk to people as numbers. My name is Dave. What's your name?

Rep: Uh, Elvis.

Me: Well, howdy Elvis. For my records, what is your employee ID number?

Elvis: You can trace me through the reference number.

Me: Golly, Elvis. You know my Social Security number and my unlisted phone number. Please tell me your ID number.

Elvis: (Real fast) 5759349649.

Me: OK, repeat that back real slowly because I am going to write that down.

(Elvis repeats it back, all the while thinking about how you are holding him accountable.)

Me: Good. Now where is your call center located?

Elvis: I'm not allowed to say.

Me: Why is that, sir?

Elvis: Security.

Me: Elvis, I live in a gated community with security cameras trained on my doors and windows. I understand security. But really, please tell me: What country are you in?

(He answers. Make sure, in response, you don't ask about the weather or what time it is over there. Don't pull back thinking you have invaded his privacy. I mean, he gave YOU a fake name!)

Me: OK, Elvis, 5759349649 in New Delhi, this is the second time I'm calling to get my refund. So before I go ahead, let me tell you that last month I talked to Sheila in the Philippines. She is 5759346739. She promised to fix this and she didn't. Do you know her?

Elvis: No.

Me: Oh, that's right, you are in different countries. Anyway, she promised to fix this and she didn't, so Elvis, here's what we're going to do. This is the last time I am calling this number before I take my complaint to the government authority. And I want you to know as a courtesy that I am taping this call for customer quality control.

Elvis: (After an audible gasp and long pause.) Oh, that's OK, Mr. Lieber. Is it pronounced Lee-ber or Lie-ber?

Suddenly, he cares! And it's off to the races. You don't have to tape the call. He won't know. But it certainly gets his attention. He knows that you know who he is and where he works and that you are holding him accountable.

Later in the book, Watchdog Nation will share more about how to tape these calls.

Your Power Sheet

Sometimes when we learn that a company is overcharging us, we get anxious and angry. Our heart races. We storm to the telephone to call and protest—and we turn to whatever scrap of paper is closest to take notes, like a Post-it note or the back of an envelope.

Watchdog Nation wants you to start your records on a clean sheet of paper. We call it "The Power Sheet" because it gives you the power to take control of your problem from the start.

NAME OF COMPANY/DATE

Customer service rep name:

Employee ID number:

Location of call center:

Time of call:

Summary of conversation:

Follow-up action by you:

Follow-up action by company:

Other notes:

Watchdog Nation Core Principle #3:

Find the company's point of vulnerability—and let it know

Remember that whatever problem you may encounter, you are not the first person to deal with it. Although you feel you are the only one facing this dilemma, there rarely is a problem that is unique to you.

Only a few years ago, you couldn't find out who else had the problem and what was being done about it.

Now, in a matter of seconds, you can learn how others have coped and if there is any official action available (a product recall, a class-action lawsuit, a government investigation). Often, the solution is quickly available and you don't have to waste your time pretending to be another unknowing customer.

You can learn the one fact they don't want you to know. Then cut to the chase:

Me: Elvis, I see that the Missouri attorney general is conducting an investigation into this, and your company may have to pay a fine. Before I get involved with that, can I talk to a supervisor?

Supervisor: How may I help you?

(You get the supervisor's name, employee ID number, location of call center and then …)

Me: Miss Smith, I want to be fair and give your company a chance to help me before I take this to the Missouri Attorney General. I see they are taking complaints now on this very problem. So Miss Smith, I'm hoping we can resolve this in this phone call, which by the way, I'm taping for customer quality control.

There you go! You just gave that supervisor the justification she needs to give you back your money.

Before you contact the media, contact the company

I'll soon share with you how to pull off the ultimate nuclear option against a company: Try to interest the media in doing a story. But before you pull that trigger, you should exhaust all other possibilities. You start with customer service representatives. You document each call and who you talk to. When you don't get immediate satisfaction, you call again and gamble that you will get a more sympathetic and caring customer service representative willing to take ownership of your problem.

No luck? Then you ask for a supervisor.

If that doesn't work, you seek out the supervisor's supervisor.

In the old days, that used to work. But not so much anymore.

Companies don't seem to care as much about their most important asset: you, the customer.

How you present your case is crucial. The best presenter I've seen is Rick Conley. He came up with a simple system to explain his problem in a clear way to DirecTV. When I asked him how he learned to speak in such a concise manner, he answered that he works as an air traffic controller. That makes sense. These folks have to say a lot of information in a very short amount of time.

Conley's problem was that his new high-definition TV receiver didn't work properly. DirecTV sent him a refurbished one, but he didn't want a pre-owned model. He never activated it, canceled the service and was billed $238 for early termination. His account was turned over to a debt collection agency. His calls to customer service, at first, went unheeded.

Here's how he presented his problem:

Main problem: Early termination fee, disputed and then turned over to bill collectors.

What happened: I upgraded to high-def receiver. The install went badly and the new receiver didn't work. A refurbished receiver was sent to me (but never activated), but after all the problems I told them to terminate my service. I returned all equipment and was billed $238 for early termination for high-def service, which I never received.

What I did: I had to finish the install myself, then spent several hours on the phone with customer service (what a joke the customer service is). I disputed the early termination charges with the dispute department only to be turned over to a bill collector.

History: I was a DirecTV customer for approximately 10 years. Problems started when I moved and upgraded to high-def.

What I want: Credit for the early termination fee and the bill collector notified. Any and all credit references cleared.

The air traffic controller was cleared for landing. His problem was solved.

Clarity is the first step toward a solution. Always ask in exact terms what you want as a resolution.

"Satellite dish – you are clear for customer service landing."

TIP: How to pitch the Media

When all else fails, it's time to approach the media.

AT&T spends millions on advertising. But one critical story can undo a lot of positive paid-for public relations.

If you have a story of corporate incompetence, write it as clearly and concisely as you can and seek out editors and reporters at your daily newspaper. Try your weekly newspapers and TV news stations, too.

Pitch the story as an example of the kind of frustrations that people face every day. Let's share the best way to pitch a story.

Reporters and editors respond best to great stories. Stories have to have a dramatic arch that touches readers in an emotional way. Classic stories have heroes (in this case, sympathetic victims) and villains.

In Richard Ellis' beef with AT&T, the victim was his 82-year-old mother. It doesn't get much better than that. Who can't sympathize with the elderly? They've lived a long life, paid taxes, raised a family, and now they get twisted up in knots while some corporation they've done business with for years suddenly treats them as if they don't exist.

Here's how someone in a situation similar to Ellis' can interest the media in doing a story.

Dear Mr. Lieber,

I want to ask you to consider writing a story about my 82-year-old mother. She has gotten the run-around from AT&T for months. We've called and called and nobody will take ownership of the problem. Unfortunately, this seems all too common these days.

In a nutshell, she is getting charged for someone else's phone bill. Her area code is different from the other number; otherwise, the rest of the number is the same.

We've called many times and have documented a record of who we've called and on what dates. We get pushed from one office to another.

But it gets worse: Now she is being harassed by a collection agency and her credit rating will get hurt.

Please help us. You can call me at my home or my cell phone. Or you can e-mail me. Here is the contact info: xxxxx.

Sincerely,
Richard Ellis

Keep in mind that pitching the media is a long shot. For every two stories I write, I reject 50. I ask myself: What makes the best story for readers? Did the "victim" do everything possible before contacting me?

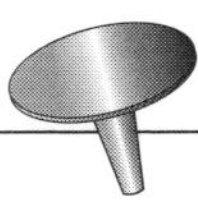

A man I admire, Nido Qubein, a speaker, college president and enlightened entrepreneur, says: "Having a flock of happy customers is like having your own advertising agency."

He writes in his Executive Briefing e-newsletter: "A major study by a commission of business experts found that the typical happy client will tell three friends or business associates about you." Word-of-mouth advertising through satisfied customers influences people to buy a product or service more often than all other forms of advertising put together.

"Don't relax too much. The study also found that people who are unhappy with you will tell, on average, nine or 10 friends. Negative comments are even more effective in destroying business than positive comments are in building it. It takes nine or 10 positive comments to overcome one negative comment."

Call me an idealist, but I can't stop thinking about one of the inventors of modern customer service, Leon Leonwood Bean. L.L. Bean's Golden Rule, the 100% Satisfaction Guarantee, has been around since 1912 when L.L. sold his first pair of Maine Hunting Shoes.

The way we were

"Sell good merchandise at a reasonable profit, treat your customers like human beings, and they will always come back for more."

— Leon Leonwood Bean

His philosophy:

A customer is the most important person ever in this company—in person or by mail.

A customer is not dependent on us. We are dependent on him.

A customer is not an interruption of our work. He is the purpose of it.

We are not doing a favor by serving him. He is doing us a favor by giving us the opportunity to do so.

A customer is not someone to argue or match wits with. Nobody ever won an argument with a customer.

A customer is a person who brings us his wants. It is our job to handle them profitably to him, and to ourselves.

If it weren't for AT&T, the electric company would be No. 1 in annoyance

In the old days, the electric company—or the power company or the light company (whatever your grandmother called it)—well, they were the good guys. Power was cheap. Customer service was friendly and on point. You rarely had a problem.

Now the electric company generates the most complaints from my readers.

Consider the case of Peggy Maurer and her *Twilight Zone*-like experience dealing with TXU Energy, headquartered in Dallas. She had a question about her electric bill, but she could never get an answer. As her monthly electric bill soared one recent summer, she learned about TXU's Energy Aid program, which provides small discounts to the poor, the disabled and older adults like her. She wanted a piece of the action.

"I don't know about you, but I need to stay cool," she says. "I have high blood pressure, and I'm on a walker. I cut off the air conditioning to most of my house except for three rooms. And even with my fans on the floor, my bill still runs about $180 a month."

She called TXU's toll-free customer service number and told the person who answered that she is in Texas.

"What is Texas?" the TXU representative asked, according to her recollection.

"It's a state," she replied. "You're not in the United States, are you?"

"We're not allowed to say," the man answered.

Maurer pressed him about his location until he finally acknowledged that her call had been routed to an outsourced call center in the Philippines.

Because he didn't know about the Energy Aid program, the man suggested that she call the number on the back of her electric bill.

She dialed, but within moments she was talking to someone from the Philippines again.

She asked her question—and was put on hold for 30 minutes.

"I almost hung up," she recalls. "But I wanted to see how long they keep you on hold. I think they want you to hang up."

When the TXU representative came back on the line, she asked, "Did you find out anything?"

"No."

"Let me talk to your supervisor, but don't put me on hold."

"I won't."

But he did.

Again.

After 15 minutes, Maurer's call was disconnected.

"I'm a persistent old thing," she explains, "so I called again."

She asked to speak to a supervisor. But she was put on hold for an additional 25 minutes.

When a supervisor finally came on the line, Maurer repeated her question. But she heard no response.

"Are you still there?"

"Yes."

"I'll tell you what. Just answer me, hon. I've been on the phone for an hour or more."

She explained her problem again.

"Hon, what are you doing?" she asked the supervisor.

"I'm listening to you."

"Hon, all I need is either a yes or a no. Are you there?"

"Yes, I'm listening to you."

"I figure your silence means no."

So Maurer hung up.

Then she made one more call. And, unlike TXU, I didn't put her on hold, ask her where Texas was or disconnect her.

Maurer and I talked about her problem. I told her that TXU Energy signed a 10-year, $3.5 billion contract with a French company, Capgemini Energy. In what was called one of the biggest outsourcing deals ever made, Capgemini took over TXU's customer-service call centers.

Before the deal, TXU's call centers were in Irving, Waco and Houston. When the deal was announced, Capgemini's chief executive at the time, Chell Smith, said her company would not send any TXU jobs overseas.

That promise was not kept.

"Some work did go overseas," a Capgemini spokesman told me later. Capgemini ran call centers in Bangalore, India; Krakow, Poland; the Philippines; and Guatemala.

TXU is in a competitive environment and needs to cut costs. But at what cost to customers like Peggy Maurer?

"Actually, I'm very angry with it," she says. "I try to be sort of nice to them on the phone, hoping I'll eventually get somebody who can get me an answer. But we do not get the service we need."

A TXU spokeswoman calls Maurer's experience trying to get an answer "pretty bad."

"First, we do apologize," the spokeswoman says. "Anytime any of our customers has a bad experience, we want to know so we can make any necessary changes."

At my urging, a TXU official called Maurer. What did she tell him?

She recalls saying, "Here you all are, messing with things that really matter. This is a matter of life and death. People need electricity for their oxygen and things like that. And we have to deal with people from the Philippines?"

When you get the run-around from a customer service person, ask to speak to the supervisor. Tell the supervisor that you want to file a formal complaint. Otherwise, your voice won't be heard when they tally up the number of complaints. ■ Keep a record of whom you talk to. Ask for his name and employee ID number. Make him spell his name. Repeat the number back. ■ Consider recording the phone calls to verify that you are not making up the circumstances. ■ When you do reach someone, give her your phone number and ask her to call you back if you get disconnected. ■ Don't give up. That's what they want you to do. ■ When all else fails, threaten to cancel your service. You'll immediately get moved to the front of the line. Customer retention is the key to profit.

MADE IN CHINA
I dunno.
It might
blow up!

TIP: Find the right person

If you don't get help when you talk to a customer-service representative OR a supervisor, here is another tactic to use.

Use sites like www.zoominfo.com or www.Hoovers.com (not free) or LinkedIn.com to track down e-mail addresses and phone numbers for company executives.

Also, go to the company's Web site and look for "News" and "Press Releases." Often the company spokesperson's contact info is in small print at the bottom.

Or try different search engines, such as Google.com, Bing.com or Dogpile.com. You can "break in" to a fortress-like company by finding an entry point such as its media relations or corporate communications department. Search for "ABC Energy spokesman" or "ABC Energy Media Relations" or "ABC Energy Corporate Communications."

Something will pop up: a news story, a press release, a social networking page, a list of Rotary members that will give you the name, phone or e-mail address of the person who is paid to make the company look good in public. Now it's time to get in touch. But what do you say?

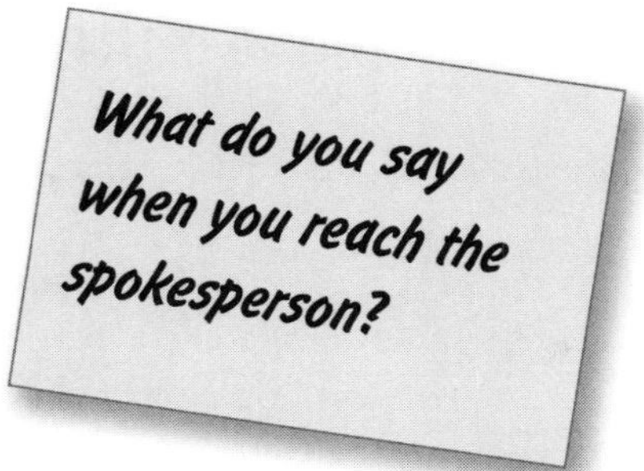
What do you say
when you reach the
spokesperson?

"Hello, Mr. Lieber. I see you are a spokesman for ABC Energy. I've been a loyal customer for more than 20 years. But lately, I've had a problem that I can't solve, and I've tried calling and writing over and over. But no one seems to take ownership. I'm at a loss. A good friend of mine knows someone who works for the local newspaper, and she suggested that I take my story to them and ask them to write about it. But my parents always taught me to be fair. I thought since you are the spokesperson for the company, and this problem could eventually end up on your desk by way of a reporter's phone call, well, I thought I would contact you first. I'm sure you know who could help me. It would probably be better for both of us if this didn't get into the media anyway. Don't you agree? Can you help me?"

Too bad Detective Columbo retired before e-mail

Sometimes, you have to play detective to figure out somebody's e-mail address, but it's worth the chase.

The president of the telephone company is going to do everything he can to hide his e-mail address. Wouldn't it be nice, though, to send your problem to his BlackBerry?

Sometimes, you can make an educated guess. You can probably figure out e-mail addresses for any company if you find a list of executives at a Web site such as Zoominfo.com or in a local business-news publication. Then you find out the company's e-mail format (by searching and using the @ sign in your search) and match the name to the format. Is it:

DaveLieber@ABCEnergy.com

or

Dave.Lieber@ABCEnergy.com

or

Dave_Lieber@ABCEnergy.com

or

Dlieber@ABCEnergy.com

About the only thing that can throw you off is if middle initials are required.

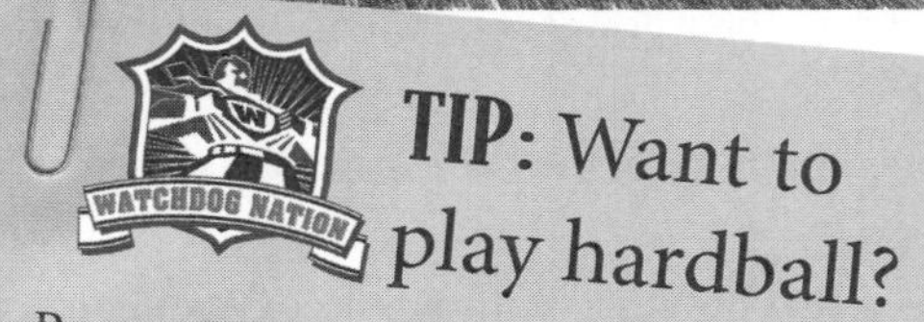

TIP: Want to play hardball?

Research the names of the members of the board of directors and send them e-mails or snail-mail letters, too. Nothing worse than when a member of the board contacts the CEO. Ouch.

Cutting the power off even though it's illegal

Little upsets me more than when an electric company cuts off the power to sick people who need electricity to sustain their medical equipment. In most states, it's illegal, but it still happens all the time.

Emily Ragsdale, 90, is a good customer for any company. She pays her bills early and uses automatic bank drafts. Because her state—Texas—deregulated electricity providers, she took advantage of a better deal and switched to Stream Energy.

Everything was fine for the first few months. That's important to Ragsdale because she has had two open-heart surgeries and sleeps with the aid of an oxygen tank.

But one hot night, electricity stopped streaming into her home. She said there was no warning of a disconnection.

"It was a surprise to me," she says.

She called her daughter, Wanda Smith, who lives a couple of blocks away. Her daughter rushed over and found Ragsdale walking through the house with her walker and a flashlight. They checked with the neighbors. Their power was still on. Then they checked the electrical box. No fuses were blown.

They called the phone numbers on the back of Stream's electric bill, but "you can't talk to anybody at night," Smith says.

Ragsdale went to sleep that hot night without her oxygen boost. Food in her refrigerator and freezer spoiled.

The family complained to Stream and showed that the bill had been paid. The company apologized. Stream waived the reconnection fee, gave her credit and even paid for the spoiled food.

Ragsdale told the company about her oxygen tank, and Stream promised that her electricity would never get disconnected again.

But three weeks later, her power was turned off again without warning.

"The second time, it caused a lot of distress," Smith says. "It probably made me madder than anything ever had, dealing with any company anywhere."

Paul Thies, Stream's marketing and communications director, tells me the company didn't credit her bank draft, even though the money was taken out of her account. Twice.

"It was our error," he says. "She shouldn't have been disconnected. It was a transactional situation glitch."

He adds, "We have 300,000 customers, and this is an anomaly. It's not like a systemwide thing."

But after the first "glitch," Ragsdale should have had an additional safeguard.

State rules prohibit an electrical provider from disconnecting the electricity of the ill and disabled, even if they haven't paid their bills, when the customers have shown that loss of electricity would worsen their health.

Individuals who qualify are supposed to fill out a form with a signature from a doctor or nurse.

Ragsdale and her family didn't know that. But even without the form, a top Stream official says, the family's notification of her health status after the first disconnection should have been enough to prevent any further disruptions of service.

Ragsdale told me, "I just hope it doesn't happen to somebody else."

Most states have laws that prohibit terminating the power for residents who need medical equipment powered by electricity. If you know someone who qualifies, make sure he or she followed the rules to qualify. Usually, the person must file a form with the signature of a medical professional. ■ *Also, in most states, if you qualify for this and fall behind on your payments, the energy company must offer you a deferred payment plan. The company is not allowed to disconnect you! Most older adults do not know that.*

What's worse? The hail—or the roofers that follow?

It was an indictment for him, and a turning point for me.

Shawn Tatum taught me more about being a watchdog than any man I know. I write this after a grand jury indicted him on theft charges. He spent time in jail. How he got there is how I learned my lesson.

Tatum was my roofer, even though, as he once said, "I never held a hammer in my hand." We met after I asked my insurance agent whether he knew a good roofer. He recommended Tatum.

Looking back, I understand now that in my haste to avoid the complicated process of finding an honest roofer after a Texas hailstorm, I got lazy. Left myself vulnerable. But my search had problems from the start. That wasn't the first roofer I hired for the job, and it wasn't the first time I let someone actually do my roofer search for me.

See, I never did a search. For the first round, I let my neighbors search for me. After they got new roofs, I went door to door and asked who did their roof, how much it cost and were they satisfied. I went with their consensus candidate.

This first company I hired to replace my roof after the 2007 hailstorm did a fantastic job. The only problem was that the crew went to a neighbor's house instead of mine and replaced the wrong roof. Our houses share the same street number and street name, but he lives on Court and I live on Drive. The pizza delivery guys get it wrong all the time. So did the roofer.

When my confused neighbor knocked on my door that night to explain what had happened, he told me that the erring roofer demanded that he pay him by filing an insurance claim. No way!

I called the roofer. When I suggested that he take the loss on my neighbor's roof because it was his mistake, he got angry with me for interfering. I asked to get out of our contract. First, he said no. Then, I tried to figure out his point of vulnerability: What was his weak spot?

Of course! This was such an embarrassment. If I played that card, I could get him to change his mind.

"How many roofs are you doing in my subdivision?" I asked.

"More than 300," he replied.

I told him I would type up the story of what he did on a flyer and tape a copy to every one of his plastic lawn signs in my neighborhood. All his customers would know that he didn't pay for his own mistakes and that he didn't even answer his cell phone when his crew went to the wrong house.

How do you like them apples?

"Guys like you make me sick," he said.

I repeated: Will you let me out of my contract?

He answered, "I never want to speak to you again!"

YESSSS!

Note to Self:
The next time I want to take a shortcut, remind myself about roofers. Roll up my sleeves and spend an hour doing proper research.

Blessed with a second chance, I knew I had to do the right thing. After all, I am The Watchdog columnist for the *Fort Worth Star-Telegram*. I tell readers how to do the right thing in these kinds of situations.

I imagined the checklist: a) check a roofer's name with the words ripoff and scam on the Internet, b) check the Better Business Bureau rating, c) ask the city permit office if the roofer is a regular customer, d) check references, e) get bids, f) check membership status and reputation at the local roofers association.

All that sounded great. For about five minutes. Then I remembered how much serious work I had to do for other people and their problems, and I wondered if I could shortcut my own. People often take shortcuts on important decisions. Looking back on it later, we realize it. But when you come to that fork in the road and take the wrong path, well, maybe that's why roofers get away with so much.

I figured out the one person in the world who had a stake in me getting an honest roofer: my insurance agent. I called him and asked for a recommendation.

My agent told me he referred all his customers to Shawn Tatum Roofing. I knew the name.

Lawn signs in my neighborhood showed the phone number and also a sign-topper: ASK FOR BUCK.

I called and asked for Buck. Not long afterward, Buck, Tatum's charming, silver-haired sales director, showed up and mesmerized me with his pitch.

This is the point in the sales process when you should say, "Can we talk by phone in a few days?" and shoo the salesman away. Then you turn on the computer or call the reference desk at the public library and begin asking questions: Does the company show up on the Internet? What does the Better Business Bureau say? Is it a member of any state associations? Are there references from past customers?

Hindsight. I know.

I signed the contract and gave Buck my insurance check. (Please note: Never give your insurance check to someone before he has done the work!)

Two months later, after hearing nothing from the company, I called and asked for Buck.

You can guess the answer:

"Buck don't work here no more."

So I talked to Tatum, an Orson Welles look-alike who promised to do the job but explained that there were delays. First, it was the rain, from three months before. Then a month later, he had a manpower shortage because there was so much roof work.

Turns out he was giving the same speech to a hundred other customers. He was taking their checks — and cashing them at a gas station. (He didn't like banks.) But he wasn't doing the work.

After months of excuses, Tatum called and told me he was sending a crew out to finish the job. (This time, roofers came to the correct house.) I later learned that I was one of the lucky ones. Only a few got service. Now every time I look at that roof, I think of the victims who will never see a dime.

In 2007, Tatum filed for bankruptcy, listing $671,000 in debts. The 86 creditors included homeowners, suppliers and subcontractors who did the work for the man who never held a hammer.

One client, Helen Webb, an elderly widow, spent two hours with Tatum at her kitchen table.

She wanted to hold the $1,700 insurance check in a bank account, but he persuaded her to let him have it. "He said he would do my roof next," she recalled. Her certified letters to him were returned, marked refused.

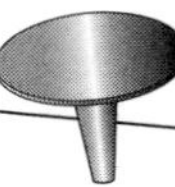

WATCHDOG NATION NOTE:

Before buying a service, remember to run through the Watchdog Nation steps:

a) Check the company's reputation on the Internet.

b) Do likewise at the Better Business Bureau.

c) Check with your city to see if the company gets required permits.

d) Ask to check the company's insurance policy and consider calling the insurance company to verify.

e) Find out who the supplier is and call and ask if the company pays its bills on time.

f) Does the company belong to a trade association?

g) Get bids.

h) Check references from previous customers.

The list of creditors — on which my name is mistakenly included — offered a road map for investigators, who sent letters to everyone. "It has come to our attention that you may be a victim of a criminal offense committed by Jerry Shawn Tatum," the letter said.

Sixty people responded with stories of how Tatum owed them either a roof or money. From them, 17 cases were strong enough to take to a grand jury, which returned an indictment alleging theft of more than $100,000.

In 2010, he pleaded guilty to theft and was sentenced to six months in jail, 10 years probation, restitution payments to victims and community service.

"The sheer volume" of that many jilted customers shows a pattern of theft, the prosecutor said.

During a 2008 bankruptcy hearing, Tatum testified that he always intended to perform the work.

Dan Pitts, former president of the North Texas Roofing Contractors Association, says customers shouldn't give contractors money before a job is started.

"I would say our average roof job is $8,000 to $10,000, and we get no money upfront," Pitts says.

"It's hard to get someone back to your house when you owe them very little money," he says. "It's hard to get them to respond to your phone calls. But if you owe them money, they're much more apt to return your phone calls."

For me, the lesson learned was to stop relying on the advice of others and instead take greater responsibility in my decisions. My insurance agent apologized to his customers. But I don't blame him. He was an indirect victim himself.

Note to Self:

My biggest mistake was letting others make my decision for me. My neighbors made the first selection of a roofer, and when that went wrong, I let my insurance agent decide the second time around. Stand up, Dave!

In a sense, after this, my roles as a newspaper watchdog and vigilant consumer merged into one. Coming close to losing thousands of dollars taught me to take nothing for granted. Everybody needs to be a detective. All the time. On everything.

*In some states, roofers need to be licensed. Check it out. ■ Roofers can get certified by roofing contracting associations. Search for your state's association and look up potential roofers. ■ Ask friends for references. ■ Get at least three bids. ■ Do an online search of the owner's and company's name to see what reports come up. ■ Check with the Better Business Bureau. ■ Check your city's rules on roofing permits. Make sure your roofer complies. ■ Don't sign anything until you completely understand the terms. Try to include a cut-off date stating that if the work isn't completed by then, the contract is void. ■ Never pay a deposit of more than 10 percent of the estimate or $1,000, whichever is less. ■ Don't make a final payment until you're satisfied with the job. * Never pay cash.*

This is how The Watchdog Nation stops a classic scam

Your bank, your credit card company and other financial companies you do business with will never send you an e-mail or call you on the telephone to ask you for personal information. The e-mail may look good, and the caller may sound good, but forget it. These are con artists.

The same goes for the Internal Revenue Service, but because the IRS deals with everyone—and let's face it, the IRS is scary—those e-mails and phone calls are more likely to be believed. Hey, it's the IRS! And they are offering you a refund or a rebate.

Of course, it's not true.

More likely, it is someone from a foreign country working his way through the telephone directory calling you and knowing your name and your phone number. Sometimes these calls even show up as from the 701 area code in North Dakota.

Bill Byrd got a call telling him to expect a check from the U.S. Treasury for $2,500. The caller—supposedly IRS Agent Sid Johnson—knew Byrd's name and address. All he needed was Byrd's bank name and account number, and the money would be transferred immediately.

"I told him to send the check in the mail, and he hung up," Byrd tells me.

Martha Kapper got a call from "IRS Agent Nick Carver" who wanted to send her a $2,400 rebate. He knew her name and address and wanted her bank name and account number.

"I told him to call me back, and when he did, I didn't answer the phone," she says.

Shirley Vess answered the phone and heard that a $2,000 rebate check was supposedly sent to her months before. Did she get it? When she answered no, the caller wanted her checking account number for a direct deposit. When she asked for the IRS phone number, the caller said he was not allowed to give out the number. (Sounds like AT&T, doesn't it?)

Curtis Arnold told the caller who promised a refund, "Great, send me a check." The caller insisted that he could be paid only by direct deposit. "The more I insisted on a check," Arnold says, "the more he insisted on a direct deposit. I got tired of the game, told him I knew it was a scam and hung up."

Leah Hogue got her good news in an e-mail with the subject line stating, "IRS Refund Notification—Message ID: 92054568." She clicked the button in her e-mail and found a Web page that looked like the authentic IRS.gov Web page. But unlike the real one, this one asked for her Social Security number, phone number, name, address and bank information.

"I didn't do anything," she told me.

Bravo to all these smart people. They are learning the way the world works in the 21st century. They are true members of The Watchdog Nation.

If you ever get a suspicious e-mail from someone claiming to be with the IRS, forward it to phishing@irs.gov. Or call 1-800-829-1040 ■ Filing a tax return is the only way to get a refund. There is no separate application form.

Your 1040 info may be all too EZ to steal

I called several people around the nation whom I didn't know and told them what was on their tax returns.

I told Peter, an electronics technician in New York, that he earned $8,676 in 2005 and expected an $815 refund.

I told Robert, a Pennsylvania construction worker, that he earned $24,833 in 2004, and that in 2005 he asked that his $2,119 refund get sent directly to his checking account.

Andrew and Elizabeth, a married couple in Connecticut, jointly earned $67,638. Their tax return lists the names and Social Security numbers of their daughters, too. The couple donated to their church ($500), an evangelical organization ($25) and a Bible club ($25).

How do I know that? In a little-known security breach that is becoming more prevalent as more Americans use their computers to do their taxes, more returns can be downloaded like music or videos.

When I explained this to Peter, Robert, Andrew and Elizabeth, they had no idea!

Computer consultant Scott Green showed me how to go to shared files on the Internet. Where people usually store music for public downloads, I could search for "1040" or "tax return" and download actual returns.

I didn't download those forms myself, mainly because I don't want to install peer-to-peer—or file-sharing—software on my computer. To illustrate the dangers, Green downloaded the tax returns and e-mailed them to me. He discovered the security breach while legally downloading files from other computers. Instead of typing the name of a song into a search field, though, he typed "tax return."

Instantaneously, a listing of tax returns available on computers nationwide popped up on his screen. He typed in a few more commands, and the tax returns began downloading to his computer.

"I was totally blown away," he told me.

The returns he sent me were found on computers in which the users did not place their personal information into secure file folders on their hard drives. Instead, they left their tax returns available in open folders, available to anyone who uses file-sharing software.

If you use one of the many available file-sharing programs on your computer to find songs or videos, you download those from others' computers with users' permission. In return, they can download songs or videos off your computer. It's considered by some to represent the sharing nature of the Internet culture.

But sometimes computer users don't realize that all files in an open folder—like bank statements and checking account and medical records—are also available if they are not moved to closed and secure files.

Jay Foley, executive director of the San Diego-based Identity Theft Resource Center, says information available on most tax returns is enough to perpetrate identity theft. The tax returns I had, for instance, showed the name, address, phone number, Social Security number and, in most cases, the bank's routing and checking account numbers where refunds are supposed to get sent.

Foley says a valid name and Social Security number is worth about $25 on the black market. Add a valid address, he says, and the value jumps to about $50. The information can be used not only to obtain a credit card, he says, but also to get a mortgage or buy a car or boat.

In some cases, Foley says, the information is not sold but traded for illegal drugs.

WATCHDOG NATION
TIPS: Computer users should make sure that when they install file-sharing software, they place open-to-share files in one folder. Sometimes, people mistakenly make their entire hard drive's contents available. ■ Copy sensitive documents onto removable media like CDs, DVDs or thumb drives, and then delete those files from your hard drive.

The moving man who didn't keep his promises

John Bjorkman, a Navy employee, thought he was doing the right thing when he hired Kevin Queppet to move his belongings from one house to another. After all, Queppet was a firefighter. His company was called Firefighter Metro Movers. And firefighters are ranked near the top of lists for integrity. They will put their life on the line for you and your family.

Queppet got the job for several reasons. Bjorkman was in a bit of a hurry. Queppet offered the lowest bid—only $800, compared to quotes of $1,100 and $1,200 from other companies.

"OK, we like firefighters," Bjorkman remembers thinking at the time. "Especially since 9/11, people see firefighters and think, 'Wow, these are our heroes. Anything we can do to help them out is a good deal.' "

But the movers who showed up were not firefighters. Queppet employed men who were not in the fire service. The movers did not finish the job in one day as promised, but they said they would come back the next day. But they didn't and Bjorkman was forced to finish the moving job himself.

In the days that followed, Bjorkman noticed damage to several items. A leg on a small refrigerator was broken off, leaving the fridge lopsided. A washer had a new ding on the side. His wife's sewing desk broke into irreparable pieces. A bag of fragile possessions was apparently dropped and shattered.

Damages came to $2,760. When he called and wrote Queppet, the firefighter didn't respond. When he filed a written insurance claim with Queppet's company, there was no response to that either.

I wish I could tell you that everything was made right. But that's not what happened here.

Even before Bjorkman hired him, the state of Texas had tried for three years to catch up with the firefighter. The state had revoked his mover's registration after he didn't respond to a customer's complaints and skipped out on mediation. The state also fined him $2,500, but he didn't pay. And the state requires movers to carry liability insurance, and Queppet neglected to do that, too.

Queppet even neglected to respond to Better Business Bureau complaints about him.

Bjorkman learned his lesson. He was in such a rush that he quickly took the lowest bid—without checking around. He liked the image of a firefighter saving him from the chaos and uncertainty of his family's move to a new home.

All Bjorkman had to do was check with the state agency that regulates the moving industry. If he had made a quick phone call and asked someone to run Queppet's name and company through the database, he would have learned about the firefighter's previous troubles. A quick call to the BBB would have provided the same information.

Don't always take the low bid. ■ *Check with the state agency that regulates the industry. In this case, the moving industry is regulated by the state transportation department. Who knew?* ■ *Before hiring a company, check with the regulators and find out about past complaints. Ask if there are any outstanding fines and if all requirements are fulfilled.* ■ *Make that quick call to the BBB, too.*

Not doing homework can cost on car repairs

When the transmission on Alexis Geisel's car broke, she found herself tested.

Geisel, who lives on her own and works two jobs in addition to pursuing her studies, did some Internet research and found an area transmission company—24Hour Auto Repair in Denton.

The owner, Larry Duncan, told her that the repair would cost less than $1,000. He said, she recalls, that he would try to get the car back to her in two days. She liked that because she needs the car to drive to her jobs.

The shop's Web site offers transmission repairs for "$997 and up" and indicates that most work is completed within 48 hours.

She signed the work order, which, she says, did not have a cost estimate. (The actual cost of the repair was later written on the order by an employee, she says.)

In the days that followed, Geisel encountered a series of delays, excuses and unreturned phone calls. Nobody would give her a complete explanation of what was going on and what the final bill was going to be.

Finally, after three weeks and a bill that jumped to nearly $2,600, she got her car back. She complained to me.

I called the owner. Duncan declined to speak specifically about her case.

"We quote the exact price before we make repairs," he said, in contrast to Geisel's claims. He can't guarantee that cars are fixed in two days, only that he will try, he added.

Geisel found Duncan's business on the Internet. In addition to his auto repair business, Duncan also states in his Yahoo! Profile that he runs an Internet marketing company to help promote the repair shop. He owns the names for several transmission-repair Web sites that offer toll-free numbers that forward customers' calls to his shop.

If Geisel had spent an extra few minutes on the Internet running Duncan's name, business name and business address through search engines, she would have learned more about the business.

She would have found Better Business Bureau complaints in which, except for one, Duncan did not respond. A check of public records shows that there were at least seven judgments against him at the county courthouse, totaling $20,000.

What should Geisel have done? Cindy Sulsar of the Better Business Bureau of Fort Worth recommends getting bids from multiple repair shops in writing before authorizing work. On a part such as a transmission, which has to be dismantled before a diagnosis can be made, she suggests getting a ballpark figure in writing before the car is touched.

"You can get the hourly labor rate, too," she says.

Before she could get her car back, Geisel was told she had to pay the $2,566 bill in cash. When I asked Duncan why, he explained: "Any time we have problems with a customer, we require cash only. They stop payments on checks."

He added, "I can tell you something: I've been in the car business a long time. People get angry because the car is broken first of all, and they just feel like somebody ought to fix it for less money. Always. But these parts cost a lot of money."

And hassle.

Get referrals about reputable car-repair shops from friends and family. ■ *Check with the Better Business Bureau for the shop's record. Search the Internet for complaints.* ■ *Get estimates for parts and labor in writing.* ■ *Make sure the repair order states that the shop will contact you for approval for any additional parts or repairs.* ■ *When you pick up your car, ask the service manager to explain all work completed and all replacements made. Get details on warranties of various parts and labor in writing.*

Don't make assumptions; they get you in trouble

I was searching for a promotional product for Watchdog Nation and settled on a great idea. A fake lottery ticket.

It looks real. You scratch off the numbers and you win a lot of money. You celebrate. Then if you're a true citizen of Watchdog Nation, you turn the ticket over and read the fine print: "Winning tickets of $10,000 or more must submit claim form by mail. Claim forms are supplied by Santa Claus. All winning tickets must be validated by the Tooth Fairy and conform to her game rules. Winning prizes may NOT be claimed anywhere, so forget about it! All winners are losers and must have an excellent sense of humor."

What a great way to show people how to read the fine print.

I shopped around. Found several Internet sites that offered the (un)lucky tickets. One site was cheaper than the others. Bubba's Wholesale. Bubba's price was $29. I paid with a credit card through PayPal, the Internet payment service that offers a Resolution Center for problem sales.

A month later, there were no lottery tickets. Bubba didn't answer his e-mail. So I went straight to PayPal and filed a dispute.

PayPal investigated. Bubba answered PayPal and then wrote me these words: "We apologize, however an email was sent out shortly after you placed your order, letting you know that the fake lotto tickets were on backorder for a few weeks. The email was returned to us as undeliverable."

I didn't believe that. Even if what he wrote were true, why didn't he respond to my e-mail asking where my tickets were.

I got my money back.

Lesson: Don't always buy at the cheapest price. Check the ratings and reputation of the seller. Whenever possible, pay through a service such as PayPal that provides a backstop.

Those lessons were driven home again a few months later. An ink stamp I used to process check payments was drying up. On top of the stamp, a promo stated that I could reorder at www.calistar.com.

When it came time to buy a replacement, I went to that Web site, which still existed, and paid $16. I assumed that because I bought it there once, I could do so again. But the stamp did not arrive. I began to worry because it contained my name, bank's name and account number.

Did a quick Internet search and learned that two years before, a woman posted a notice that she had sent money to Calistar for a replacement, and she never heard from the company again. Oh, if I'd only read that.

I returned to the Web site and dialed the phone number. The phone was disconnected. I sent an e-mail to the company, and it was never answered.

So I launched into action by "flooding the zone" with complaints. First, I filed a complaint with the Better Business Bureau in Sacramento, Calif. The company had an unsatisfactory record and failed to respond to 16 listed complaints. If only I'd checked that before buying.

I complained to the local sheriff's department in California where the company was situated. They told me to complain to my local police department, which I did.

I complained to California Attorney General Edmund G. Brown Jr., whose office promised to write the company on my behalf. I also informed the federal Internet Crime Complaint Center (IC3), which wants to know about Internet fraud (www.ic3.gov). And I ordered another stamp from somewhere else.

A few months later, a plain brown envelope arrived from California. There was no note inside, but it contained my stamp.

By then, though, I had already complained to my bank, which promptly restored the funds without any hassle. Now I have two check stamps—one for each hand, I guess. And another lesson learned. Don't assume that any company behaves the same now as it did in the past. Check it out.

The law you need to know about

Here's a homework assignment for you. Go to your personal computer (or public librarian who can do it for you, if you don't have a PC) and type this in your favorite search engine: the name of your home state and the words "deceptive trade practices law."

What you will find is a gift from the consumer gods. Read your state's law and quickly see how so many horrendous business practices we take for granted are actually illegal. But authorities need a complaint to go after the perpetrators.

Here are some excerpts from my home state of Texas:

No person may disseminate a statement he knows materially misrepresents the cost or character of tangible personal property, a security, service, or anything he may offer.

No person may knowingly make false or misleading statements of fact concerning the need for parts, replacement, or repair service.

In some states, your law might be called a consumer protection law. Whatever its name, this particular law, for The Watchdog Nation, is the gift that keeps on giving.

Captain George flies head first into scams galore

George Kahak probably shouldn't be allowed near his mailbox.

The mail that comes to his Fort Worth home promises the former chief pilot for American Airlines what he wants most: more money.

After 40 years of flying, Kahak retired, but he put much of his retirement money in bad investments, including some with a financial adviser who went bankrupt.

Now 85, he looks for ways to stretch his remaining dollars. Each day, he reads his mail and studies the promises of prizes, giveaways, easy work-at-home jobs, investment opportunities and whatnot.

So much sounds believable, he says, marveling, "Boy, they've got some good writers." His wife, Margaret, tells him not to do it, but he doesn't listen.

He says that in the past few years he has made "investments" in two dozen entities, spending anywhere from $10 to $7,500. He acknowledges that he loses every time. Still, he can't stop himself. He is looking for that golden goose.

"He's such a sweet guy, so good-natured that he would give you the shirt off his back," his wife says.

That's exactly what he's losing. But Kahak is the first to admit that he can't help himself. Financial exploitation of the elderly is pervasive, unyielding and growing alongside technology that makes it easier to perpetrate scams, the Federal Trade Commission reports.

Kahak is an extreme example. But unlike most older Americans who are embarrassed to talk about their losses, Kahak says he wants to share his story so others can understand what he is now beginning to see:

Nothing comes easy.

We met one day after he asked for help sorting through his mail for a legitimate proposal. Seconds into his mail pile, I knew it all was too good to be true. A sampling (in the hustlers' own words):

"A stock that triples every month for six months no matter what the market is doing."

"The secret to getting free money now."

"Put $50,000 in your pocket in just 30 days."

Many of the envelopes carry Kahak's handwritten notations about the date he mailed in money.

He fell hard for letters that said he won a prize: "They make it sound great," he says. " 'Your check is already made out to you. Just send in the fee. We'll send you the check.' But that's the last you hear from them."

He is mired in a pyramid scheme: "Your name is on the bottom, but when your name comes up, you make all this money," he explains. "The guys above me are making $800,000. It sounds beautiful." Alas, he's stuck down low.

He's an oil man: "This one outfit is going to drill in Alaska, and I'll clean up. They own so many hundreds of thousands of acres right where the oil is. And they made it sound like pretty soon I was going to make money on that. I haven't made a penny."

He paid to learn how to win the Powerball lottery: "I don't think I ever heard anything from them."

He spent $39.95 for a system showing him how to be a millionaire: "They get your money, and that's it."

"I'm just a glutton for punishment," he says sheepishly.

His biggest investment is his worst.

Two representatives called him to sell him a yearlong commitment to an Internet advertising company.

Their company, New Age Marketing Solutions of Phoenix, promises to create Web pages for him that act as "affiliates" of more established companies like Amazon and eBay, they said.

Kahak doesn't own a computer and doesn't surf the Internet. But that didn't matter. "Those guys really talked me into it. They were telling me that everybody orders off computers."

The price was $14,000 to join, but they liked Kahak, he recalls them saying, so they cut the price by almost half.

"They really sounded honest. It was just before Christmas and they said, 'Oh man, you're going to make a pile before Christmas on Yahoo and eBay.' "

He didn't listen to his wife. He spent $7,500 to cover his first year for Internet advertising.

His earnings since then?

Zero.

I called the company. Supervisor Kimberly Johnson told me, "If he knew the business wasn't right for him, he shouldn't have signed up for it."

He can cancel and receive a refund of $108, which represents his signup fee, she said.

What about the rest of the $7,500?

"The advertising cost is not refundable," she said.

The Better Business Bureau in Phoenix lists the company as having a satisfactory rating.

Kahak is thinking about getting a job now, preferably a home-based one because, after a recent stroke, he walks with a cane.

The offers for those jobs come in the mail, too.

"I called that outfit that puts toys together," he says. "They pay you $500 a week. That's a couple of thousand a month. I may do that."

John Haun, a case manager at Senior Citizen Services in Fort Worth, says older Americans sometimes need help to overcome their losses and learn how to protect themselves.

"It's like being a gambler," he says.

He suggests that conversations with telephone solicitors begin this way:

"Before we go any further, I need to know your name, name of your company and your phone number so I can call you back." Legitimate companies will comply.

Haun adds: "If you want to do business with someone, you look them up in the phone book, you call, and you know what you're doing. If somebody calls you out of the blue, you don't know anything about them. You're at a huge disadvantage."

George Kahak promises to stop being the ultimate mark. But he doesn't sound sure.

"I just about quit doing it anymore," he says halfheartedly. "I just keep hoping that something will come through, but nothing ever does."

Watchdog Nation Core Principle #4:

Ask a bunch of questions

This is my favorite core principle because I firmly believe that Americans are always two or three simple questions short of learning what we need to know. We stop asking questions too soon.

Look at the Great Recession of 2008-09. Supposedly, our financial system unraveled because of the housing boom, built on overinflated prices and buyers who couldn't afford what they were buying.

Did anybody ask a bunch of questions?

Did the homebuyer, sitting across the table from the lender, ask: "Hey, I see this is an adjustable rate mortgage. Can you tell me what my payment will be in five years, and what will happen if I can't make them?"

No, the homebuyer was thinking about the granite kitchen counters, the sunken living room and fireplace, the expansive back yard. The American dream come true.

Did the lender, in turn, ask, "Hey, looking at your salary here, I'm wondering if you'll be able to afford the mortgage payment, taxes and insurance when the adjustable rate mortgage goes up in a few years. Do you want to hold on and talk about this before you sign?"

No, the lender was eyeing his prey and the blank signature lines on the settlement papers. His thoughts? "If I can get this family to sign, that will be the sale I need to put me over the top in the sales contest. I can take my wife to Hawaii!"

Whoopee.

And how about those Asian and European investors who bought, sight unseen, billions of dollars worth of mortgage-backed securities? Did they ask a bunch of questions about whether the properties involved were actually worth the inflated prices tied to them?

No, they thought they saw an easy way to earn profits. But of course. . . .

Until recently, it was difficult to figure out what questions to ask when buying anything. But now, the questions you are supposed to ask before buying health insurance or athletic equipment or a house are usually found within seconds on the Internet. So, too, are the answers you should be looking for.

Others have done much of your research for you. It's important to remember this so you can take advantage of this vast ocean of previously uncollected knowledge. Now it's all out there in the world's free library.

Even something as simple as purchasing a cup of coffee at Starbucks should be researched. You think I'm kidding?

When you walk into a Starbucks, how many sizes are on the menu?

Three.

Large, medium and small.

Or, as Starbucks says to confuse us, venti, grande and tall.

Me: "Hi, I'd like a small, please."

Barista: "Oh, that's a tall."

Me: "No, I want a small."

Barista: "That's a tall!"

Who's on first. What's on second. I don't know is on third.

But did you know there are three secret sizes at Starbucks?

If you checked the Internet before buying, you'd know more.

Internet search: What's the secret size at Starbucks?

Press ENTER.

Answer pops up in 1.3 seconds.

There is one five-letter word you must say to the barista to get the secret size. It starts with an "s":

S _ _ _ _.

The Starbucks Coffee Menu

Everybody knows about these sizes: (from left), venti, grande and tall.

Short.

It's smaller than a tall, usually costs 10 to 20 percent less than a tall and offers more than enough of Starbucks' legendary caffeine buzz.

But I'm not done.

The Secret Starbucks Coffee Menu

Hardly anybody knows about these sizes: (from left) short, sample (free) and sample Frappuccino (also free).

There's another word in the English language that gets you a FREE cup of coffee at Starbucks.

Internet search: How do you get free coffee at Starbucks?

ENTER.

1.2 seconds later: Ask for a sample.

You can get most drinks for free in a sample cup. Well, almost all except for a frappuccino. Why not a frap? Because Starbucks has a different cup for a free sample of that.

So, in truth, Starbucks actually offers six different cups, but only lists three on the public menu. The fourth is smaller and cheaper. The fifth and sixth are actually free.

Amazing.

Disgusting, too.

Why doesn't the company tell us everything we need to know to help us make smart buying decisions?

Watchdog Nation believes the company wants you to make dumb buying decisions that benefit its bottom line. Buy more coffee than you need. Pay more. Don't try a free sample when you can pay full price.

The point is this: If buying a cup of coffee at Starbucks is so darn complicated, imagine what it's like when you buy something more costly, like a new refrigerator, a long-term life insurance policy or an appliance repairman's services.

They are not going to give you the information you need to know to make a smart decision. It's up to you to figure it out.

When was the last time your cell phone company called you and said, "Mr.

Smith, this is your cell phone company. We were looking at your rate plan, and we see that based on the pattern of your calls, if you switch to our new billing plan, your bill will be cut in half. Interested?"

No, they don't tell you. Of course not.

But if you ask, they have to tell you.

Here's an easy way to slash dollars from your family budget right now. Pull out your monthly bills, call the companies and ask for lower rates. Tell the credit card companies there is a mistake on your interest rate. It's too high. Chances are at least 50/50 that the company will lower your rate simply because you asked.

Tell the phone company that the cable company has offered you an incredible deal on phone service but before you switch to its arch-enemy you want to give it a chance to lower your bill. Ask for a "recession discount" or a "senior discount" or a "hardship discount." Tell one company about the other's better deal.

Ask a bunch of questions. Your bills will drop bunches of dollars.

Frustrated at the lack of information people have before they make decisions, I spent my own money to print a thousand yellow buttons that urged:

Ask a bunch of questions.

The buttons were hugely popular. In fact, I only have a few dozen left.

Candidates wore them to election debates to remind voters that they would not automatically say yes to whatever proposal was put before them.

Consumers put them on kitchen bulletin boards as a reminder about how they ought to deal with service techs who came to make repairs.

Journalists taped them to their computer monitors to remind them of their mission.

USA Today *even wrote about the button.*

But to me, it's more than a slogan for a button. It's a way to protect yourself as a member of The Watchdog Nation.

One of the biggest Internet scams of all time

I'll bet you $79.95 that you never heard of "Your Money Machine Success System" or YMMSS. That's how much money you would have lost if you signed up for this Internet investment scheme, even though the promise was you would double your money every two or three months.

Turns out YMMSS is one of the biggest Internet scams ever.

As far as I can tell, until I wrote about it 2006, no journalist had ever covered the story. But the story was huge on the Internet where disgruntled investors gathered to share their stories at an amazing Web site devoted to exposing scams of this nature—www.MatrixWatch.com.

This proves how important it is to do a search on any business opportunity before you invest in it.

The program was supposed to reward investors who promised to view Internet advertising for 30 minutes each day. They would get a percentage of ad sales supporting the Web sites they visited if they wrote product reviews and provided feedback to advertisers.

Critics called it a pyramid scheme.

When it finally shut down in 2007, the company said it had 24,000 investors in 143 countries. No doubt they would have had more if not for the exposure on the Internet.

Multilevel marketing plans, also known as network or matrix marketing, are a way of selling goods and services through distributors. You receive commissions both from sales and by recruiting others to join. ■ *Most state laws declare these pyramid schemes illegal under deceptive trade practices laws.* ■ *Beware of plans that ask you to recruit others, the Federal Trade Commission says.* ■ *Distrust opportunities that offer enormous earnings.* ■ *Insist on taking time to think over your decision. Talk it over with family members, knowledgeable friends, an accountant or a lawyer.* ■ *Do a background check by searching for information at the Better Business Bureau and through Internet search engines.*

Ask a bunch of questions about that toilet!

If something in your house is broken and you can't get it figured out, the only thing to do is ask questions. Sounds obvious, but…

After I moved into my house more than a dozen years ago, the toilet in the guest bathroom started showing its temperamental side. Over the years, that pesky little toilet demanded more attention than my kids. Yearly, I poured gallons of chemicals down that drain, plunged it so much that I became a master plunger and, not for kicks, bought my first auger, or drain snake. (You should have seen me try to put that baby back in the box.)

Yet I could never figure out the problem, let alone fix it. We usually had an unattractive sign on the door that warned, "Don't use this bathroom."

But when I assumed leadership of The Watchdog Nation, I began learning about character traits that ought to be displayed by smart consumers. If I practice what The Watchdog preaches, I wondered, could I finally solve this problem?

My incentive to find out grew stronger in December when the troubled toilet hosted a pre-Christmas blowout. Its cleansing waters overflowed, sending a small stream cascading across the wooden floors of several rooms. I was the only guest at this party.

I quickly ran out of towels. A water cleanup company was called in. Eventually, my homeowners insurance paid $8,000 for replacement flooring.

In the weeks that followed, though, I made mistakes in judgment that cost me money but left me with no solution.

The first thing I should have done was seek a full-fledged plumbing inspection. But instead, I gambled on the idea that the toilet was the problem. I bought a new one. Cost with installation: $595.

That gamble looked good for a month, but then the new toilet began showing symptoms of its predecessor's madness.

The next step also cost money and still didn't yield a solution: I asked my home-warranty company to send a plumber. He charged me $45 for the visit before announcing that the problem was most likely caused by an off-center toilet. The warranty only covers a block in the drain, he said.

An off-center toilet, I learned, is one where the in-floor pipe and the toilet's drain do not properly meet. When you look down the pipe, you only see half a hole; the rest is obscured by its off-centeredness.

Plumbers say this happens because some builders don't want a toilet too close to a wall or a cabinet. So they install it off-center, away from the hole.

Some people who know me would say the only throne I deserve is an off-center one.

The plumber offered a quick fix of resetting the flange—a gamble not covered under the home warranty. I put down $160 on his gamble. But I lost. Moments after he left the house, the toilet returned to its troublesome ways.

I called the plumbing company, which didn't return the call for days. They finally called to say that for another $475, they'd put in another part that "might work." When I protested, they agreed to give me a $160 credit toward the next purchase.

If this doesn't work, they said, we could jackhammer the floor.

I never used the $160 credit. My Watchdog experience kicked in. My instinct, which I decided to listen to for once, told me that something was wrong. Stop pouring good money, a little voice told me, down a bad drain.

So I called the plumbing company that originally helped build the house in 1994. At the very least, they could see the results of their handiwork.

A crew of two arrived. One plumber wore sunglasses—indoors. The other wore a baseball cap.

Ballcap and Sunglasses said they were sure the off-center toilet was the problem. They removed the toilet, but surprisingly everything looked good.

That's when I started asking a lot of Watchdog-type questions. (But I asked them quickly because their rate is $90 an hour.)

"Why don't you check the drain to the street? Can you put a snake into the toilet? How do we know it's not an obstruction unless we go in there?"

Eventually, I insisted that they use their auger for a better look.

Wearing rubber gloves, they pushed the auger into the drainpipe. Ballcap, holding the flashlight, said he felt something about a foot down.

Ask a bunch of questions.

"How skinny is your arm?" Ballcap asked Sunglasses.

"Not skinny enough to go down there," Sunglasses answered with alarm.

"See something?" Sunglasses asked Ballcap as he peered down the drain with a flashlight.

"Yes, I do!"

Ballcap poked a copper pipe into the drain. Like a fisherman, he pulled out his prize: a broken piece of PVC pipe. That little obstruction—I measured it later at 3 inches by 2 inches—had sat in the drain, flopping around, for a dozen years.

Since President Clinton's first term, that pipe fragment pivoted within the larger pipe. "It was operating just like a gate," Ballcap said.

Ballcap theorized that the original plumber who cut the pipe dropped the piece into the drain.

When I reminded him that their company was most likely involved, Ballcap joked in defense that "sprinkler guys use PVC, too."

Ballcap called the home office to explain. When he returned, he said, "No charge. We stand behind our work."

I admire the company for doing the right thing. It doesn't happen enough. Not much different from asking lots of questions. That doesn't happen enough either.

Work at home? Chances are you'll pay upfront costs and never see your money again.

Nancy Jenkins answered an ad and signed up to work at home, but once she sent in the required $337 to get started, she never heard from the company again.

"That's when I started calling and calling and calling," she told me.

"I was very nice. I left my name and phone number and said, 'It's been three months since I sent in my money to your company. I have called, e-mailed you, faxed, and I've not had any response. Please return my phone calls.' "

When I looked into it for her, I found there were two reasons why Jenkins' calls were not returned.

The first, according to U.S. postal inspectors, was that the Dallas-based business was a scheme, not a legitimate enterprise.

The second was that the two owners were in jail. They faced a 24-count federal indictment charging them with mail fraud.

The 24 victims named in court papers were from across the nation.

The company operated under the name A&A Insurance Forms Co.

Jenkins needed a job: "I'm a single mother. I lost my job. I even had my grandmother read their letter because she's very skeptical. When she saw A&A, she said, 'That's Alexander & Alexander.' She thought that would be OK."

But A&A has no connection with the well-known insurance company Alexander & Alexander. And the owners of this A&A turned out to be Alice Faye Turner and Malcolm G. Lincoln.

The pair, court papers show, promised that their work-at-home business, which was supposed to involve sending out insurance forms, could earn someone between $129 and $17,960 a week.

The government contends that A&A did not send insurance forms back to those who signed up. Instead, materials promoting the work-at-home business were sent, and respondents were asked to send them to others.

The ploy was successful. Postal inspectors conducting surveillance of A&A's post office mailbox reported that, "Due to the volume of mail, their mail would not fit in their post office box and had been placed in a large tub with a note directing them to the window to pick up."

A police sergeant watched as Lincoln carried a box from the company's office to a Dumpster. After Lincoln disposed of the box's contents, the sergeant retrieved them and gave them to postal inspectors. The contents included letters stuffed by people who signed up with A&A. (People sent letters back to the company for postage to be added so they could be mailed.)

"In the end," court papers state, "the complainants never received any money in return."

Use extreme caution when responding to ads that promise a salary if you work at home, the Better Business Bureau warns. ■ Never pay a fee upfront for any service. ■ Never give out bank account or credit card numbers to anyone soliciting for such businesses over the phone. ■ Some companies require you to pay fees for materials involved, but projects may take longer to complete than promised. Some companies only pay for finished products that are deemed acceptable. ■ Before you sign up, check out the company with your local BBB and also at www.bbb.org, the national site.

Travel clubs? It's better to stay home.

The young man on the telephone promised my wife and me a trip to either Las Vegas or Orlando or a cruise to Cozumel if we attended a 90-minute sales presentation.

"Is it free?" I asked.

"Uh, yes," he replied before adding, after further questions from me, that I would have to pay taxes and port fees on the trip.

The next Sunday we attended the session at American Voyager Travel offices and learned how we could join a "private, full-service travel club" for $7,485 and travel for the same discount rates that a travel agent pays.

Our salesman told us that if we joined, we would become "associate agents" with the company.

He showed us his ID card and said we would get cards just like his with the words "Travel Agent ID" above our photos.

He showed us the many travel bargains we could expect because "you're a travel agent."

A former employee of the company told me later, "They're taking people's money and not giving them anything in return."

Another ex-employee told me, "They're selling air. The salesmen all say that. There's nothing tangible. It's a membership in a travel club that makes you look like a travel agent."

At that seminar, I kept telling the salesman no. He dropped the price down from $7,485 all the way to $2,485. I still said no.

But I did expect my free trip. I decided to go to Vegas. I sent in the required $50 deposit and waited and waited.

When they finally contacted me about the trip, they offered the most inconvenient dates to travel. Plus, they intended to put me in a motel near the Las Vegas airport.

I never got to go.

But I did make a visit to the company's corporate headquarters in Dallas.

On a tour, I watched as a staffer created an identification card, marked "Travel Agent ID," for a customer.

When I told one of the company owners that the Texas attorney general had forced another Texas-based travel club to stop telling customers that they were travel agents, she replied, "We have to revamp the wording."

Don't fall for sales presentations that promise free trips as a reward. ▪ *Never agree to sign a contract with a travel club immediately after a hard sell by a company salesman. Take the contract home, read it carefully and show it to a lawyer, if possible. If the salesman says the offer goes away if you don't sign immediately, don't fall for that ploy. That's a real warning sign.* ▪ *Travel clubs are risky. Some people who sign up for them say they regret doing so later.* ▪ *Always check the club out on the Internet and with the Better Business Bureau.*

Watchdog Nation's Near Guarantee

This is probably Watchdog Nation's best advice about how to stay out of trouble when it comes to door-to-door peddlers and free seminars:

Don't buy anything you weren't already planning to buy. If an asphalt crew comes by and wants to do your driveway, don't do it. If you want some driveway work, go out and hire a reputable company.

If you go to a seminar for a travel club or an investment plan, don't buy into it on the spot. Take any unsigned papers home with you and show them to family and friends.

And here comes the Ultimate Advice:

Tell the seller, "I'd like to take these unsigned contracts home with me and show my family, friends and our attorney before signing anything. Is that OK with you?"

If the answer is anything other than "Yes!" you have a problem. If he says the price will go up if you don't sign right then, so what? If he warns that you will lose add-ons, who cares? If he doesn't feel confident enough to let you walk out the door so you can check with family or friends, he is not worth doing business with.

It's an easy test to apply to any pressuring salesperson.

"I'd like to take these unsigned contracts home with me and show my family, friends and our attorney before signing anything. Is that OK with you?"

Why saying 'Good job' is important

The corporate characters in this book are so savaged in these stories that it's important to balance out the bad with the good. That's why whenever I encounter a customer service rep for a beleaguered company that I know is getting tarred and feathered by its customers, I always jump at the chance to reinforce good behavior.

I couldn't wait to send this letter to the top guy at American Airlines. (In the actual letter, I used her full name.)

Mr. Gerald Arpey
Chief Executive Officer
American Airlines
4333 Amon Carter Blvd.
Fort Worth, TX 76155

Dear Mr. Arpey,

I had a very positive experience with one of your staffers recently and wanted to let you know. On March 15, 2008, my family and I flew AA from D/FW. Due to a variety of little incidents, we ended up at the counter too late to get our baggage checked.

Alison G, who I understand is usually a gate attendant, was working the ticket counter. She worked diligently to rush our check-in. She even called the gate and alerted them that our luggage would be tagged so it could be brought straight to the gate. Thanks to her, we made our flight.

I hope you can convey to her and her supervisors how much the Lieber family appreciated her going the extra mile for us. It made the difference.

Sincerely,
Dave Lieber

Don't get too nostalgic about pay phones

When you were a kid, your mom said that if something bad happened, just call her collect from a pay phone.

Well, don't give your kids that advice unless you are very, very wealthy.

Some people miss the old public pay phones. Cell phones have made them harder to find. But there still are pay phones. When you find yourself in an emergency, you are happy to find one. These days, pay phones live up to their name.

Steve Watkins ran out of gas on the highway. He forgot his cell phone and wasn't carrying any change. He walked along the access road to a gas station, which didn't have a gas can to spare. Then he found a pharmacy with a pay phone.

Turns out, Watkins' troubles were only beginning.

He ended up using a debit card to make what in the public pay phone business is called an operator-assisted call. That makes him a favored customer in the industry because someone using an operator or a debit card requires more services and, yep, pays more for the call.

Usually a lot more.

Since Congress deregulated the pay phone industry about 20 years ago, it has become the Wild West of telecommunications. You never know what you might pay for a call.

Seeking gas, Watkins tried to make collect calls. He called the store he owns and his parents' house. But both used an Internet-based phone system that does not accept collect calls.

So Watkins pulled out his debit card and made those calls with an operator's help.

He got his gas.

Later, he saw the charges on his bank statement.

$172.90.

Watkins called Legacy Long Distance, which handles the calls for the pay phone at the pharmacy. He protested and got two of the calls removed.

He also called his debit-card company. He learned that of the charges, $75 was for a "hold" placed on his account by his financial institution. Each of the three remaining calls had a $25 hold attached to it. The actual calls were $9.58 each.

In a hold, money is frozen in your account to cover the potential amount that you might spend, usually at a hotel, restaurant or gas station. A hold is always more than what you actually spend. Holds are designed to make sure the customer has enough money to pay the bill.

Watkins wasn't expecting the holds. Because of them, he had $75 less than he thought in his account. Several of his checks bounced. More penalties to pay.

And you thought the price of gasoline was high?

Complain to the state agency that regulates the pay phone industry and also to the Federal Communications Commission about pay phone overcharges. ■ *Check your bank account regularly for holds. Know how much money you have.* ■ *Complain to the store that hosts the pay phone.* ■ *Always keep quarters in your car.*

Always be polite...

It goes without saying.

No, actually, it doesn't.

Watchdog Nation says the worse other people behave, the more likely you can be successful by acting nice.

Of course, that's extremely difficult when the person on the other end of the line on the other side of the world could care less about you and your problem.

But being nice does instill in you a sense of discipline. Nothing can get in your way. You are going to will yourself across the finish line.

Here are Watchdog Nation's tips. (If you have trouble doing these, for whatever reason, remember these work as reverse psychology.)

The worse they act, the nicer you behave.

1. Always say "Please" at the start or end of every request.
2. Say "Sir" to the males and "Ma'am" to the females.
3. Whenever they do something in your favor, say "Thank you" and add their (name to personalize it.

Here's a trick that helps me stay polite. If I tape my customer service calls, I want to sound as polite as can be so a company official who may hear the tape understands that it was his staffer, not me, who acted out of line.

Watchdog Nation's original member

Ever hear of the Greek philosopher Epictetus?

He was probably the first member of Watchdog Nation.

A former slave, he lived between the years 55 and 135 A.D.

Eppie believed that individuals have free will and absolute power over all matters within their control. He believed that we shouldn't wallow in self-pity when things go bad. We should recognize we have the power to respond.

That was a big concept 20 centuries ago. Back then, leaders wanted everyone to believe that they, not the individual, were in control of society's destiny.

Difficulties, Epictetus said, determine a person's true character. It's not what happens to you that matters, but how you react to difficult circumstances that define you. He said:

> "Make the best use of what is in your power. And take the rest as it comes. . . . If you seek truth you will not seek victory by dishonorable means; and if you find truth, you will become invincible."

You won a car! Yeah, right.

I got a blue postcard in the mail from "Awards Verification Center" with some great news:

"You are an official prizewinner in our NEW MERCEDES, BMW, PORSCHE or $40,000 CASH promotion."

But read that sentence carefully. I am an official prizewinner in a promotion whose name has the world's greatest cars and a large cash prize in it—but that doesn't mean I actually won a car or the cash, does it?

The postcard goes on to dangle "a luxury 4-day Royal Caribbean Cruise," "a $1,500 Shopping Spree" and other prizes. All you have to do is call a toll-free number "to visit and claim your prizes."

You know me well enough by now to know that I checked it out.

The postcards come from Silverleaf Resorts, a Dallas time-share resort company that owns 13 resorts and is listed on the American Stock Exchange.

Sandra Paredes, the company's director of owner services, said that about 100,000 "happy owners" bought at least one week a year in one of the company's condos that sleep six people. The average purchase price is about $12,000.

Yeah, I know, you want to hear about the luxury car.

Turns out that in the 20 years Paredes has worked for the company, no one has ever won the car. But it's not what you think. Winners are given a choice of either a car or $40,000 in cash. They always take the money, she said.

You get your prize after you listen to a 90-minute sales pitch, she said, and use a scratch-off card to see what you win.

She sent me a long list of winners from the previous three years; there are almost 250 names on the list. I called several of them, and they verified that they had won the prizes listed.

Without real winners, the company would violate the Texas Timeshare Act, a state law that governs the awarding of prizes for time-share promotional marketing. The law says it is illegal to offer a prize and then not award it.

So what are the odds of winning?

To win the car or the $40,000 cash prize, Paredes says, the odds are 1 in 53,130.

To win $1,500, the odds are 10 in 53,130. To win $500, the odds are 20 in 53,130.

Nearly everybody else wins a four-night stay billed as a "romantic island holiday" in either Aruba, Hawaii, Jamaica or Puerto Rico, Paredes said. But winners are responsible for airfare, food, gratuities and taxes—meaning the actual prize is the hotel stay.

Plus, she said, all receive a trip to Orlando or Las Vegas for two nights that includes airfare and accommodations, but there are restricted dates, and you must depart on a Tuesday.

The Better Business Bureau listed 138 complaints in three years against the company, but many were resolved. The Texas attorney general's office says there have been 49 written complaints against Silverleaf in the past two years.

If you research a company on the Internet that offers prizes, you may find dozens of anonymous complaints against the company, mostly related to confusion about the prize offerings. ■ *The Better Business Bureau advises about some companies: "If you received an award letter from this company, it does not mean that you have won a contest. You will receive a free gift if you attend the sales presentation, but the chances that you will receive a major prize such as a car or cash are very slim."*

Identity theft: Does the government really care?

Identity theft is one of the leading causes of complaints at the Federal Trade Commission. Millions of Americans are in fear of it happening. Millions more, like me, have already had it happen to us.

Here's the sad truth: You can't count on the government to protect you when you are the victim of identity theft. There are too many victims, and law enforcement hasn't made it a top priority.

Yet ID theft can cause you years of frustration and a loss of money that you can't recover.

States are enacting tougher ID protection laws. Now all ID thefts reported to police must be handled with written reports, but that doesn't make the problem go away. And people still have trouble getting police to take reports.

Charles Clay, a 78-year-old heart patient, learned these lessons the hard way. He received a letter from his cardiologist's office telling him that "our office was burglarized and our entire computer system was stolen. Please alert your credit bureau about possible identity theft."

Nothing like that kind of news to make your heart beat faster than it should.

A panicked Clay tried to call the major credit bureaus to check his status.

"I found out it is almost impossible to speak to a human being," he says, explaining he got lost in the bureaus' automated telephone systems. "I never got to talk to someone about identity theft. It was a rather frustrating experience for me. I felt like I needed help and didn't know where to go.

"They'll have my Social Security number, which is certainly not a good feeling. Of course, they'll have my address. I don't want to wait until it's too late and say, 'Gosh, I should have done something.' It pays to be proactive, and that's what I'm trying to be."

Here's what I told Clay to do: Put a fraud alert on his credit with one of the three main credit bureaus (Experian, Equifax and TransUnion). A fraud alert lets you know if anyone is trying to open any accounts using your name or other personal information.

Clay also needs to start monitoring his credit report to look for evidence of wrongdoing. And if he finds any examples of purchases he didn't buy, he should notify one of the three bureaus immediately. (One bureau is supposed to notify the others, but that doesn't always happen. Consider contacting all three.)

But what if Clay doesn't want to do all that? And what if he wants to protect himself before ID theft occurs? In recent years, a new identity-protection industry has developed in which others say they will do the work for you—for a fee.

Insurance companies offer other identity theft coverage. These policies typically offer coverage that includes their staffers contacting credit bureaus for you; making emergency phone calls to creditors, banks and other agencies; assisting you in replacing documents; and providing emergency cash advances—in some cases up to $25,000—in recovery reimbursement with no deductibles.

Some insurance companies even offer emotional support with a licensed behavioral specialist.

One of the leading companies in this burgeoning industry is LifeLock. Company founder Todd Davis is so sure that his company can protect you that he shares his Social Security number as proof. He's not scared about ID theft. For the record, his number is 457-55-5462.

LifeLock places a fraud alert on your credit—and renews it automatically every three months. This means that if you—or anyone else—tries to open a credit account in your name, you first have to give personal approval with a phone call. The caller asks you personal questions that only you know the answer to. One example: What was the address you lived at 14 years ago?

I used to be a Lifelock customer, but in 2010 Lifelock agreed to pay $1 million in restitution to eligible customers. The Federal Trade Commission and 35 states charged Lifelock with misleading and deceptive practices. After this, I switched to another company, Debix.com

And what happened to heart patient Clay? After I contacted LifeLock about his case, the company gave him free coverage for life.

"Gosh, that's good news," he said.

ACCESS TO ALL
FILES AND PASSWORDS
CLICK

TIP: ID theft help

You can use www.annualcreditreport.com to request a free credit report from one of the three major credit reporting agencies every three or four months. To place a fraud alert or a credit freeze on your credit information, contact one of the bureaus:

Equifax
1-888-766-0008
P.O. Box 740241
Atlanta, GA 30374
www.equifax.com

Experian
1-888-397-3742
P.O. Box 2002
Allen, TX 75013
www.experian.com

TransUnion
1-800-680-7289
P.O. Box 6790
Fullerton, CA 92834
www.transunion.com

For more information on how to protect yourself, visit the Federal Trade Commission Web site at:

www.consumer.gov/idtheft/

Another great tool is the Identity Theft Resource Center:

www.idtheftcenter.org

You can also consider putting a "security freeze" on your account. A security freeze means that your credit file cannot be shared with potential creditors or potential identity thieves. Various states have different laws. Go to www.financialprivacynow.org and click on "How to get a security freeze in your state" to see what the law is where you live.

How I handled my ID theft

On the final day of 2008, I got a phone call, but it wasn't someone with good wishes for the new year. The call was from a woman at a collection agency. She was stern and to the point: She asked me to repay $279 for a bounced check I had written at a Wal-Mart in Pearland, Texas.

Only I have never been to Pearland, and I don't write checks at Wal-Mart.

My first thought: scam.

I asked for her company name, and she told me. When I asked for her name and employee ID number, she refused, saying, "You'll get a letter." She hung up.

I did an Internet search for the company name — TRS Recovery — and the words Wal-Mart and bounced check.

A slew of comments came up.

One person reported a similar situation: bounced check in a Wal-Mart he never visited, and he doesn't write checks.

His bank representative, he wrote, looked up TRS on the Internet and discovered that the company "is a fraud!" He complained that letters from the company "looked very real" and worried about people who have been "scammed by this company." He added that he intended to file a police report against the company and also a complaint with the Federal Trade Commission.

After reading that and similar comments on another Web site, I thought that was all there was to it, and I could return to prepping for our New Year's Eve celebration.

But a voice in my head asked, "What would The Watchdog do next?"

An unexpected twist

Next I checked the company's Better Business Bureau report online.

What I found was unexpected and further proof that a lot of people write a lot of nonsense in blog postings. Was this a scam? Hardly.

Turns out TRS Recovery is an affiliate of TeleCheck, which operates an electronic check verification system for retailers.

The BBB report shows 677 complaints against the company. Half are for billing and collection issues. But another statistic is one not found in a scam company. Of those 677 complaints, the number resolved is also 677. This is a company that cleans up its messes.

The free report listed company officials with phone numbers. I picked the top name on the list and called her – Denise Hossler, director of compliance. It was New Year's Eve. I figured I'd never get anyone. But Hossler answered her phone.

She offered to help, and no, I didn't tell her I'm the leader of Watchdog Nation. I wanted to see how she treated customers. I got lucky. This is someone who cares. When I complimented her on the perfect BBB record, she said that was her personal goal for the year.

Hossler looked up my file, and we figured out what happened.

Someone had bought $279 worth of merchandise at a Wal-Mart in Pearland using a fake check with my name and address. The check purported to be from a Harlingen credit union.

I was the victim of identity theft.

Happy New Year.

A victim again.

What did Yogi Berra supposedly say? Deja vu all over again.

Thirteen years ago, I tried to pay at a Wal-Mart, and the store declined my check. Turns out someone had written a check at a Montgomery Ward store in my name. Later, I learned another check was written at a toy store.

Back then, it took longer to clean things up. For two weeks, I wasn't permitted to write checks. A state trooper told me that my driver's license number was probably "pulled out of the air" by a con man.

Very few people become the victim of ID theft twice, says Linda Foley of the Identity Theft Resource Center. "You've been hit twice."

Better that than lightning.

According to one study, Americans have a 1 in 37 chance of becoming an ID theft victim.

In Texas, a legislative study showed that although half of all Texas ID theft victims lost no money, they spent between four and 130 hours fixing problems related to the theft. For those who did lose money, losses averaged $500.

My state has laws to protect people in my situation. A debt collection company can't hold me responsible for a debt I didn't incur. Lenders can't penalize me if I apply for loans or credit.

But what concerns me is the ease with which someone can pull this off. Fake checks — called synthesized checks — can be printed on a home computer.

I wondered about Wal-Mart's procedures for verifying checks. Wal-Mart spokeswoman Ashley Hardie told me that check writers at Wal-Mart stores are randomly checked for additional information such as a driver's license or a phone number, but this only happens when a cashier is prompted to ask for more information by the TeleCheck system. That means not all customers' checks are verified.

Mike Prusinski, a spokesman for LifeLock, which provides loss protection for consumers, said big retailers that don't demand more rigorous check verification are a major contributor to identity theft.

"If Wal-Mart and all the other places, instead of doing it randomly, did it all the time," ID thieves would face tougher obstacles, he said.

Foley, of the ID Theft Resource Center, says, "Thieves know which companies don't check things carefully and which ones do. They're not stupid. This is their profession."

Next, I'll show you how I dug out of this hole.

After identity theft, know how to fight back

I didn't let this ruin my New Year's fun. I wasn't angry or upset. I didn't panic. I figured that whatever happens, I can deal with it. Then I tried to make as many calls as I could to learn what happened and do what I was supposed to do before the clock struck midnight.

I followed my Watchdog Nation training.

It doesn't take long to lay the groundwork to protect yourself when something like this happens. I kept a diary of my experience, and I'll share it so you'll know what to do if this happens to you.

1. I check out the collection agency – TRS Recovery – on the Internet. I discover that others have received similar calls. Several write that the TRS/Wal-Mart/bounced check story is a scam and that the company is taking money from innocent victims. But that turns out not to be true.
2. At the Better Business Bureau Web site, I learn that TRS is an affiliate of TeleCheck, a large check-processing company. The company has a perfect BBB record. 667 complaints. All of them resolved.
3. The BBB report lists phone numbers for company officials. I call the first one on the list — the director of compliance. Even though it is New Year's Eve, Denise Hossler answers her phone. She walks me through the facts, and I learn that this is a case of identity theft.
4. At her urging, I call workers at TRS' fraud unit to register a dispute. I get a reference number. They tell me to get a Federal Trade Commission ID theft affidavit form from www.ftc.gov, fill it out and fax it to them to wipe the slate clean.
5. After downloading the affidavit from the FTC Web site, I complete it and take it to a notary. Notary public Stephanie Silva hears what has happened and says of ID thieves, "If they spent as much time doing honest work, they'd be millionaires."
6. I call the FTC ID theft hot line (1-877-438-4338) to register for a national list of victims. I get another reference number.

7. The credit union where the check supposedly originated tells me the account with my name doesn't exist. Someone used the credit union's name but printed the check on his or her own. The credit union sends me a letter confirming that.
8. The FTC affidavit is faxed to the debt collectors, along with the required proof of address (my water bill). But I receive no verification that it arrives. So I call back and ask for the mailing address so I can send it certified, return-receipt requested. They say that's not necessary. I do it anyway.
9. When I call the Wal-Mart store to report the theft, I'm placed on hold. Eventually, I hang up. Later, Wal-Mart's media relations department puts me in touch with a Wal-Mart risk-assessment employee, who takes a formal report. (A Wal-Mart spokeswoman says that ID theft victims should report incidents to the store involved.)
10. I call the sheriff's department that covers that Wal-Mart store to file a complaint, but I'm told to contact my hometown police department. My police department takes my complaint and gives me a police report number, which I'm told is the most important reference number of all. I'll file an open-records request with the city to get a copy of the actual report.
11. I call LifeLock, a company that provided me with limited ID theft protection for $10 a month. A representative tells me that if I lose any money, LifeLock will cover it and that if I ever have a problem clearing my credit report, the company will work on that, too.
12. At the Identity Theft Resource Center's Web site (www.idtheftcenter.org), I read informative articles about ID theft. Then I call the center's Victim Assistance Center (1-858-693-7935) and talk to an adviser. She reminds me that this is not going to ruin my life, hurt my credit score or take money out of my pocket. Most people, she says, "are very upset. They don't know what to do. They've never had this situation happen to them. They ask, 'How dare anyone do this to me?'"
13. I call Linda Foley, a leader at the ID Theft Center, to ask more questions. She recommends that I call the three major credit bureaus and put a fraud alert on my credit to prevent anyone from opening a credit line in my name. Anyone can get an alert for 90 days before

> renewing the alert, but as an ID theft victim, I can get it for seven years. She also suggests that I ask the bureaus for a security freeze so no one can access my credit report without my permission. (TransUnion, 800-680-7289; Equifax, 800-525-6285; Experian, 888-397-3742)

Foley says that as credit tightens, thieves turn to check fraud. Unlike a credit card account, which can be closed, a check writer can keep writing fake checks. Every time a fake check pops up somewhere with my name, I'll have to answer it by sending that FTC affidavit to the merchant as my explanation.

When does this end for the thousands like me who endure this? Probably when stores put in check-processing systems that show cashiers a photo, a thumbprint or some other verifier of the actual identity of the checking account holder.

The retailers won't spend the money until enough customers complain.

Bite the collection agency back

Linda LaBeau, a victim of credit-card identity theft, didn't know her rights as a credit-card holder. So she was rightfully paranoid when debt collectors started calling and telling her she owed $4,000 on her Capital One credit card.

Because of a snafu regarding a change of address, she hadn't received credit-card statements—or late notices—in months, and she had lost track of her bills. She didn't remember the $4,000 debt and figured it was a remnant of her identity-theft problem, since that was the amount rung up on her stolen cards.

She called Capital One several times asking for back statements. Every time, she recalls, she was told the statements would come. But none ever did.

Meanwhile, NCO Financial Systems, the collection agency, began calling her many times a day. She explained the situation (she was willing to pay, but she needed to know what the charges were for), but the calls wouldn't stop. She pleaded for more information, but NCO representatives wouldn't help her.

Eventually, five months after she asked for her credit statements, they arrived. She recognized the $4,000 debt as hers. But how was she supposed to get NCO to stop calling her?

Fort Worth lawyer Jerry Jarzombek says she should have sent a letter to the collection agency by certified mail, keeping a copy for her files. Under federal law, a collection agency must stop calling a person for 30 days when a consumer sends a letter disputing the debt. The collector can file a lawsuit against the debtor, but the calls are supposed to stop. If, as happened in LaBeau's case, a financial statement proving the debt is sent to the consumer, the collector is allowed to call again.

LaBeau says she got several calls every day from NCO. Under law, collectors are not allowed to repeatedly use the phone to annoy a consumer. If they do, a consumer can sue a collection agency for harassment. "Eight calls in a day are ridiculous," Jarzombek says. "If you made contact once, you should be done."

Jarzombek, who has sued NCO several times, suggests taping the phone calls for use as evidence in a lawsuit. Such recording is legal under Texas law. (Check your state.) When a collection company loses such a lawsuit, it often has to pay attorney fees for the winner.

The federal Fair Credit Reporting Act and the Fair Debt Collection Practices Act are the laws that regulate debt collectors.

By researching NCO on the Internet, LaBeau learned that in 2004 NCO had to pay $1.5 million to settle Federal Trade Commission charges that it violated federal law by reporting inaccurate information about consumers to credit bureaus. NCO also reached a nonpaying settlement with the Securities and Exchange Commission in 2005 in which it agreed to cease certain debt-collection activities.

How can consumers keep inaccurate information from being added to their credit files? File complaints with the credit-card company, the collection agency, credit bureaus and government agencies. If all else fails, sue.

LaBeau's case was solved, and she learned a lot.

"I thought I was acting as a responsible credit-card holder by contacting Capital One," she says. "I would like more consumers to push back on the tactics used by collections agencies."

Keep track of your bills. ■ When a month goes by and no statement arrives, call right away. ■ Pursue your legal rights to protect yourself from debt collection agencies. ■ Use a search engine to read summaries of the Fair Credit Reporting Act and the Fair Debt Collection Practices Act. Then act on them. ■ Contact a lawyer. You can find one in your area who specializes in this at www.naca.net. ■

TIP: Recording your calls

In some states, this is illegal. So don't do it. But in other states, it's OK. To find out what the law is in your state, go to an Internet search engine and type in "wiretapping laws by states."

Let's assume it's legal where you live. Here is the easiest way to do it. Go to an electronics store and purchase a digital voice recorder. The price has dropped considerably in recent years. Recorders have various time spans that they can record. Some record for several hours, others for a day or more.

This is important: Make sure the DVR you buy can connect to your personal computer using a USB cord. Some models have "PC" as part of their model number to signify they can connect.

Also, buy a separate recording attachment that can be used with a phone. One end plugs into the microphone hole in the DVR. The other end goes in your ear. When you hold the phone up to your ear to speak, press the record button on the DVR. The earpiece will pick up the other person's voice and also your voice.

When you are done and you decide you want to keep the recording of the call, connect the DVR to your computer using the USB cord. DVRs also come with simple software to make this transfer easy. The phone call file will transfer into your computer.

Then create a file folder in your hard drive. Mine is called "Consumer." Copy and paste the phone file into the consumer file. When you click on it, the file will play.

When I talk to a credit-card company and negotiate my percentage rate, I record the calls. If the bill arrives and the rate is wrong, I call and complain. They tape our calls. Why shouldn't we tape theirs?

Here's another example. I recently called AT&T on a matter. The phone representative hung up on me. Within five minutes, I e-mailed a copy of the phone conversation to executives at AT&T headquarters.

I'm sure it wasn't a happy day for that employee.

The Watchdog Nation. We play for keeps.

TIP: Recording your life

Wiretapping laws don't apply when you aren't using the phone. There's an ethical issue about recording your in-person conversations when others are not informed. To get around that, you can tell the other party that you are recording him or her. This is especially smart to do with salespeople. Say you do this because it's easier than taking notes and it helps you remember.

Recently, I started carrying a digital voice recorder in my car. I decided to do this after getting stopped by a police officer while driving. The officer accused me of driving too fast into a drive-through lane at a fast-food restaurant. Because it was a steep turn, I had to slow considerably. I thought he was wrong, but I don't argue with the police.

However, I thought the officer was verbally abusive for no reason. He yelled and claimed that I almost ran him over. He asked, "Do you want me to go home to my children tonight?" He was imagining things.

He didn't give me a ticket. But something about his manner scared me.

From then on, I started carrying a voice recorder. If I get stopped, I turn it on. The police are recording me, so why shouldn't I record them?

Oh, by the way, that officer eventually lost his job, in part, because of other similar incidents.

TIP: 'But I don't have the Internet'

Often people, especially older adults, will say they can't fight back because they don't have a computer, Internet access or e-mail. That's no excuse to not be part of The Watchdog Nation. There's a resource in your community available to you for free that can help you.

Your neighborhood librarian.

Don't underestimate the value of your local librarian. He or she is trained to dig up answers that most of us can't find.

You can call the library and ask for help. The librarian will look it up and call you back. Or you can go into the library and ask for help in person.

The value of a librarian was driven home to me a few years ago when my local librarian solved a problem that dogged me for several years.

I wanted to learn about the Great Train Wreck of Watauga, Texas, in 1918. But nobody seemed to know the exact date on which it occurred. One day, trying to find original accounts, I drove myself into a dizzy tizzy scrolling through microfilm of several newspapers for every day in 1918 trying to find the exact date of the wreck.

Finally, I asked the Watauga librarian. It took awhile, but she solved it. Everyone had the wrong year.

The wreck happened in 1917.

The Yellow Pages isn't always your friend

Who knew that the garage-door repair industry is one of the worst industries in America?

Don and DeAnn Carter called Discount Garage Door Co., which DeAnn says lists an address in a nearby town. She found it in her Yellow Pages.

When the repair technician arrived, the couple received a written estimate for $476. Don approved it.

But by the time the repairman left, he had charged the family more—$928. DeAnn was gone, and Don wrote a check for that amount.

She later complained to the company. The company suspended the technician for what a spokesman told me was "a very small infraction in the pricing."

But DeAnn wasn't done. First, she called other garage-door companies to get other opinions. Those other companies told her that the Carters paid too much.

Second, she checked with the Better Business Bureau and learned that the company the Carters hired was listed as having an unsatisfactory record with 40 complaints listed against it.

The more I researched the company, the more startled I was.

The company operates many different garage-door companies that all ring to the same telephone line in Dallas. The companies, according to the BBB, are: America's Choice Overhead Door Co., A-AABLE Overhead Door, AAAble Texas Overhead Door, Able Door, First Garage Door, Overhead AAA Garage Door, Superior Garage Door and Garage Door Service.

I found many of these companies listed in the Yellow Pages with different phone numbers. But when I called some of them, they rang into the same call center where the operator answered with a generic, "Good afternoon. Garage door service."

A company spokesman told me there was no attempt to mislead. Because of consolidation in the industry, "There are people out there with warranties through various different companies, and they need to find us."

The most prominent of the companies in this affiliated group, America's Choice Overhead

Door, has been cited in Georgia for deceptive practices. Specifically, the company forwarded its calls to an out-of-state call center, misrepresenting to customers that the company was based in Georgia. It failed to honor advertised price guarantees and deceptively induced customers by misrepresenting charges. The company was ordered to pay a $20,000 fine.

DeAnn Carter quickly called her bank and canceled the check for $928. She called the company and told them to bring the check back and she would replace it with one for the original $476 estimate.

When a repair technician arrived, she handed him a check for $370, stating that she was deducting the bank's $30 check cancellation fee along with another $76 to cover her time on the project.

A company spokesman told me he lost money on the repair, but that the company decided not to argue with her as part of its "goodwill gesture."

DeAnn's motivation for not giving up was simple: "I would like to see people ask questions before it happens to them."

Get written bids. ■ Check with the BBB. ■ Ask if a company has liability insurance. ■ Get a basic estimate on the phone, but expect a more accurate estimate once a repairman visits you. Get it in writing before the work begins. ■ Be on guard if a company answers its phone with a generic name. ■ Ask for customer references in your area. ■ Make sure the company's listed physical address is correct. Be wary of a company that doesn't list a physical address. ■ Don't mistake the size of a telephone book ad for credibility. ■ Don't authorize work until you understand the exact problem and the complete costs. ■ Avoid high-pressure sales tactics. Garage door repairs should rarely cost more than several hundred dollars. ■ Never pay in full upfront. Never pay in cash. ■ If possible, watch as the work is done.

Fixing the post office

Man, I was tired of the United States Postal Service.

Tired of sending letters to the correct address, only to have them returned as undeliverable.

Sick of letters and packages getting lost.

Angry that mail that should have been delivered in one or two days was taking a week.

Then I met Ellis Burgoyne. He was tired of the same things. Only he was in a position to do something about it.

He was USPS' Southwest region vice president.

When we first met, I told him the story of how someone had mailed a check to me at my correct address, but that particular piece of mail was returned to the sender—for no good reason. I called my postmaster, but he never called me back.

Burgoyne's response: "We're trying to influence that behavior. When a customer calls, we need to do the basic things, like calling a customer back and following up to make sure the solution is implemented."

He wasn't just licking envelopes.

I learned that the post office conducts internal quality checks. Mystery shoppers mail letters across postal zones, and scores are based on whether the mail arrives on time. USPS leaders like Burgoyne live and die by these scores.

Burgoyne always raises his scores, and the Southwest region was no exception.

I started collecting postal complaints from readers and forwarding them to Burgoyne's aides.

Then a few months later, I went back to the first 100 postal complainants to see if their complaints were handled properly.

To my amazement, 95 percent of the people said they were happy.

Sue Williams told me: "I've been to the post office recently, and I'm thinking the folks there may have had a 'talkin' to' because it seems a bit more congenial and helpful."

Marcia Allen, who complained about long lines and poor customer service at her local post office, told me: "The clerk appeared to have been instructed to make sure that everyone was happy. He insisted that I smile before handing me my package. It was a pleasant exchange, and I could see the other two clerks were both working as quickly as they could to move the line. So my response is positive."

Bob Mhoon said, "I consider this a very positive experience, in that most complaints to the USPS are glossed over and ignored. It was great to hear from a real person, and I was quite impressed that it was speedy, factual and candid."

This was the last thing I expected to hear. The post office? Improving?

It shows the power of leadership to change a culture. It proves it can be done!

Burgoyne says: "If you're not satisfied with the level of service you're receiving, I personally want to know about it. I guarantee you I will do everything I can. Southwest is going to get better. We've just begun."

If you have problems with mail delivery, find out who the leadership is in your postal region. ■ Call and ask for the phone number or e-mail address of the "manager of consumer affairs and claims." ■ If you can't get satisfaction, ask for the name of the region's vice president. It's a little tricky, though, because the postal service uses middle initials in its e-mail addresses. Example: david.l.lieber@usps.gov.

Four words you should challenge: "Your meter is accurate."

This probably has happened to you: The monthly bill for your gas, water or electricity arrives, and the total has skyrocketed. You call the utility to complain, but the customer service representative, without even bothering to examine your issues, simply mutters the house line: "Your meter is accurate."

I've learned better.

When Jimmie Cheek, a nurse, started getting unbelievably high water bills from her home city, Arlington, Texas, her personal pressure gauge boiled over.

She knew that Arlington was overbilling her, but when she complained, she said, the city kept putting her off.

"I almost feel like I'm the crazy one," she told me. "But I know I'm not."

Her saga began when the city gave her a new meter, one of 6,000 replaced each year.

The next month, her bill was $120 for water usage. The city claimed that Cheek used 46,000 gallons. That's a lot of water for someone who lives alone.

Keep in mind that the average Arlington water customer uses 10,000 gallons a month, according to city officials.

Her next bill showed the same 46,000 gallons for another $120. The bill after that was $123 for 47,000 gallons.

Cheek was beside herself. She doesn't have a pool. Her friends and neighbors with big families, larger yards and swimming pools were getting smaller bills.

She believed that the new water meter was faulty. She began complaining. A customer service representative told her that many people complain about higher bills after a new meter is installed, because the reading is more accurate. (A customer service representative told me the same thing when I called.)

Her next bill showed 37,000 gallons used and the one after that showed 36,000 gallons. By then, Cheek had cut back her watering so severely that a Japanese maple tree died, and her backyard holly bushes withered in the summer heat.

She hired a plumber to check for leaks. She called a sprinkler company to check her sprinkler lines for leaks. She again called the city, which twice sent crews to check for leaks. Nobody found any.

Next bill: a whopping 62,000 gallons (her highest bill, at $165). The one after that? 42,000 gallons.

When she complained again, the city sent her a flier about how to troubleshoot for leaks.

The flier infuriated her. She angrily wrote back: "I think you missed the point of my recent letter. I want an investigation of the new meter. If you would review my history of water bills and compare them since my new meter was replaced, you would understand my concern."

She concluded with a promise that enrolls her as a charter member of The Watchdog Nation: "I will continue my pursuit until I have an answer."

When I called the city for answers, I found a sympathetic official. He looked at her bills and acknowledged that they made no sense.

He scheduled Cheek's meter for an accuracy test. Within minutes of its completion, Cheek called me with good news:

"It's a bad meter. Can you believe that? I had them out here twice before. I knew it was a bad meter. I told them, 'I've been trying to tell you that.' "

Her new meter reported that she used 20,000 gallons for every 10,000 gallons she actually used. Cheek had been charged double for city water. The city refunded her money.

If your gut tells you that your bill is in error, demand that your meter get checked for accuracy. ■ *If you're not satisfied, consider hiring an independent tester.* ■ *File a complaint with the state or local agency that regulates the utility.* ■ *Keep track of all your calls and letters demanding action.* ■ *Be like Jimmie Cheek and don't give up!*

Beware of fake landlords

Here's a scam that's becoming more common as people rent apartments and vacation homes they see on the Internet without ever meeting a real landlord.

The Jolly family was looking to rent a house. After answering an ad, they met a woman named Shelly who showed them a five-bedroom, two-story house. They liked it, so at a meeting at a nearby Dairy Queen, they paid a $400 deposit and $725 for the first month's rent.

And they paid in cash.

When the time came to move in, Shelly asked the family to wait a week. New carpeting coming in, she explained.

The family drove to the house to show the children their new home. But when they arrived, there was a truck in the driveway. Must be the carpet installers, they thought.

Turns out that the truck belonged to another family who had just moved in.

"After talking with this couple," Deena Jolly said, "we found out that Shelly had rented this house out to the both of us."

The Jollys called Shelly and demanded their money back. Shelly said she would meet them at the Dairy Queen and return the money. It was all a misunderstanding, she said. Shelly showed up, but she gave the family a hot check on a closed account.

Later that day, the Jollys found out that a third family had made a deposit on the home, too.

Ultimately, according to the local sheriff's department, 10 families thought they had rented the house from Shelly, who wasn't even the owner. She was a fake landlord.

The Jollys had their worst Christmas. "She didn't just rob us of our money and our Christmas," Deena Jolly said. "She also stole our dignity."

Shelly, according to prosecutors, is actually Michelle Renee Thompson, 39, who is originally from Indiana.

A grand jury indicted her. Investigators said they believe she fled with several thousand dollars, and an arrest warrant was issued. Eventually, she was arrested. Police say she was engaging in similar activities when she was caught.

Fake landlords are a problem nationwide, says Tracey Benson, president of the National Association of Independent Landlords. "Actually, one of my employees went through that," Benson said. "She put money up without seeing the apartment. It looked beautiful online, but it didn't exist."

The scam is growing, she says, because of the increased use of the Internet to show properties. The fake landlords want the money up front, she says. "A lot of times, they communicate only with e-mail."

Before handing over money for a deposit or rent, check the tax appraisal district's database for the name of the legal owner. If you don't have computer access, ask a public librarian to help you. ■ Don't pay cash, and get receipts. ■ Never pay without going to the property and meeting the landlord or his or her agent. ■ Check the landlord's Web site, if there is one, for authenticity. Does the company or individual have a physical address or just a post office box? ■ In many states, real-estate agents must be licensed. Check. ■ Some cities require registration of rental property, so check with the city. ■ Ask the landlord what kind of professional associations he or she is a member of, and call the associations to verify.

Don't believe everything you read*

**Check the fine print*

AT&T telephone cards have introduced their own version of the new math:

1,000 equals 200.

And that didn't sit right with Georgann Trammell.

She believed that, by golly, if the prepaid phone card promises 1,000 minutes on the front, then she should get 1,000 minutes of calling time. Not 200.

Here's what happened: An AT&T PrePaid Phone Card Plus she bought at Sam's Club for 1,000 minutes wasn't working correctly. It gave her only 200 minutes for in-state calls. Bad news: There was nothing wrong with her card.

AT&T raised the rates on its prepaid cards for in-state calls. The cards still promise 1,000 minutes and do deliver that—if you call out of state.

But the cards no longer deliver a minute-for-minute trade in Texas, where Trammell lives, and most other states, because in-state access fees have been tacked on.

Note, though, that not all of AT&T's competitors in the prepaid-card business have passed these charges on to customers. More on that coming.

An AT&T spokeswoman tells me that if customers read the small print on the front and back of the card, they will see AT&T's full disclosure.

On the front, the card promises 1,000 minutes, in big numbers. But below that, in letters that I measure to be about one-sixth the size, the card states: "In-state rates may be higher."

On the back, in the middle of the purchaser's agreement, it states that for calls that begin and end in Texas, minutes may be deducted at a 5-1 ratio. That means that for every minute of talk time, AT&T will charge Texas callers five minutes.

Before you faint, be glad if you don't live in North Dakota, South Dakota or Missouri, where a 1,000-minute card buys you a mere 125 talking minutes (8-1 ratio).

In Texas, where do the other four "minutes" for each one minute of talk time go? AT&T says your money goes toward in-state access charges.

Why the change? AT&T blames a Federal Communications Commission ruling declaring that prepaid phone cards should be treated like basic telephone service. That means in-state access charges must be paid. But by whom?

AT&T says customers are alerted two other ways to the rate increases: Read about them on www.att.com or hear a voice recording when they try to add minutes to their card.

Trammell said that wasn't good enough: "Most of us don't have time to read the fine print on everything in life."

Here's what I think: A consumer who sees a phone card with a large number such as 1,000 on the front has a reasonable right to expect 1,000 minutes of telephone service.

But that's not happening. An FCC spokesman told me that consumers who believe they have been the victim of deceptive advertising should file complaints with their home-state attorney general, the Federal Trade Commission and the FCC.

AT&T says it will lower its rates if the states lower their access fees. One state, New Mexico, has already dropped its ratio from 8-1 to 3-1. With one minute of talk for a three-minute charge, that's still nothing to brag about.

Here's how I found an alternative: I did a quick Internet search and found at least one company that offers you the exact amount of minutes that are listed on the card. I called the company and asked this question:

"Do you adjust your fees for in-state calls like AT&T does, or do you offer a minute-for-minute ratio on your card for in-state calls?"

They gave the right answer. Always shop around.

Does AT&T really like U.S. soldiers?

Before Christopher Morse left to join the 101st Airborne as a private first class, he and his mother stopped at a local AT&T store.

Morse, at 34, was one of the older U.S. Army recruits headed to Iraq. When his mom, Dee, asked why he decided to join, he told her: "I've done all the fishing and hunting. I'm not married. It's time for me to do something for my country."

Morse wanted a way to send e-mails home to family and friends. So he and his mother purchased a data connect card for his laptop. The AT&T clerk promised that an unlimited data plan was available for troops going overseas for $79.99 a month.

"We went in and told the guy specifically that he was going to Iraq," Dee says. They signed up.

Morse left for the staging area in Kuwait. While there, he told his soldier buddies about his unlimited plan and offered to share. So his pals sent e-mails to their friends and family members, too.

Then the first bill arrived at Dee's home.

She opened it, looked at the final amount and shouted, "Oh, my God!"

It was for $4,953.15.

Most of it was for roaming charges.

She called AT&T to complain. The first person said he would check into it. But nobody called her back.

A week later, she called again. This time she got the verdict: Her appeal was denied. Pay up.

She called back to protest and was passed on to a supervisor.

"She said, 'I'm going to check into it. I will get back to you, I promise,' " Dee said. "I never heard from her."

She contacted her family lawyer, who contacted me.

"Then everything happened," Dee says. "I got a call from a guy with the [AT&T] president's office."

AT&T canceled the bill, waived the $175 disconnection fee and said they were sending the family two pre-paid phone cards so Morse could call home during the holidays.

AT&T does, in fact, offer an international data plan, but only to a dozen countries. Iraq and Kuwait, where Morse and his soldier buddies sent the e-mails, are not among them.

"We deeply apologize for any distress or inconvenience this has caused her and her son," an AT&T spokeswoman said.

But the problem goes deeper than that.

I mystery-shopped AT&T. I called the toll-free number for sales listed on its Web site and after 10 minutes of waiting on hold, getting transferred and then getting told to call another number (a typical AT&T customer experience whenever I call), I finally reached a saleswoman named Brenda. She said she works at an AT&T call center in Birmingham, Ala.

I asked her how much it costs for a soldier in Kuwait or Iraq to use a data connect card on a laptop.

She told me $130 a month.

For unlimited usage? I asked.

Yes, she replied.

Just to be certain, I went over the details two more times.

Each time, she confirmed that the details were correct.

"Thanks, and have a great day," she told me before I hung up.

When I told an AT&T spokeswoman what happened, she told me that AT&T regularly trains its people to offer correct plans. "However, to reinforce this message, we're using several employee communications channels to remind our representatives of the details of our international plans."

She added that when I write about this, "please do not give your readers the impression that AT&T does not care about military families, because that simply isn't true." ❧

When you talk to a salesperson about a service you are going to purchase, ask for his name and company identification number. ■ Write it down in front of him on a piece of paper, along with the terms promised you. Write the date and time, too. ■ Ask him to sign it in front of you. Keep it. ■ If he refuses to sign, take your business somewhere else. Yes, it's gotten that bad.

Welcome to
Baghdad
HOME SWEET HOME

Somebody who got it right

Times were tough at Time Warner Cable's North Texas office. I received a lot of complaints from angry customers. Did some research and learned that the company had major problems nationwide because it recently purchased another company.

I contacted the company's regional manager, Gary Underwood. He promised to work hard to correct the problems. He kept his promise, too. I stopped getting complaints.

When I first interviewed Underwood, he said something I won't forget. I share it here because, apparently, he meant every word of it:

> "I believe every complaint is a gift. You learn from that and work hard to make sure it doesn't happen again. The ultimate goal is to satisfy our customers."
>
> — *Gary Underwood,*
> *North Texas Manager,*
> *Time Warner Cable*

Dealing with harassing phone callers

The phone company won't do much to protect you when people call to harass and annoy you. Even with all the technology that exists today, the best the phone company says is, "Why don't you change your number?"

Before I share with you one way you can stop the calls, let me share the story of a 95-year-old woman I tried my darndest to help.

For months, the home phone rang most nights at her home. She picked it up and said hello. But the caller never spoke to her. She hung up. The phone rang again. Same thing. It happened hundreds of times.

Sometimes she heard background noises. She filed a police report stating that several times she heard a man making kissing noises.

"It was frightening at first, because they kept calling and I didn't know how to respond," she told me.

She kept complaining to AT&T and to the police. But nobody seemed to care.

Change your number, they always said.

But she didn't want to. She had the same number for 49 years. She was afraid that most of her friends, who are in their 80s and 90s, would lose track of her.

"I think they should be punished some way," she insisted. "This has been going on too long."

The retired schoolteacher tracked the calls for me. There was a Hitchcock quality to her log: "Calls began at 10:30 p.m. and continued as if they were on automatic redial. At midnight, I decided if I was going to have any sleep, I would need to take the phone off the hook.

"Sunday morning, today, the calls began again at 8:30 a.m. When I left for Sunday school, the calls were still coming. Tonight, at 7 p.m. they started again. Tonight the man caller kept saying 'Hi,' repeatedly, and I could hear a clock ticking. Please, please help."

AT&T recommended she get a Caller ID device.

That helped. Through Caller ID, she discovered the registered name listed for the number used by her tormentor. Calls were coming from the 936 area code. But she couldn't understand why nobody was chasing the culprit when she had found an electronic footpath to his door.

In Texas, where she lives, and in most other states, telephone harassment is a crime. Anyone who "causes the telephone of another to ring repeatedly or makes repeated telephone communications anonymously or in a manner reasonably likely to harass, annoy, alarm, abuse, torment, embarrass or offend another" is guilty of a misdemeanor, the Texas law states.

A police spokesman told me the crime is difficult to prove:

"Typically, what the detective will tell a victim of phone harassment is if they're not willing to change the number, then block the number." (In this case, an AT&T spokeswoman says a long-distance number cannot be blocked.)

"If they're not able to do that," the police spokesman said, "keep a log of the time each call occurred and start building this harassment case."

Police can subpoena the phone company for records of that particular caller.

"Usually, in the majority of these cases, once the police contact the suspect and let them know they are a suspect, the calling stops," he said.

The retired schoolteacher tried another step AT&T recommended. She dialed *57 immediately after one of the nuisance calls. This allows the phone company to trace the call and create a record that can be used by law enforcement.

Eventually, AT&T captured the number and forwarded it to the police.

Nothing was ever done.

When I called the police to inquire why, a lieutenant told me that it had fallen through the cracks. Not unusual for a big-city police department.

In the end, the woman changed her number.

Contact your police department and file a report. ■ *Use Caller ID to trace the number, as well as dialing ∗57 for Call Trace, if your phone company offers the service.* ■ *Collect evidence for a possible harassment case. Keep a pad and pen and a clock by the phone and write down the exact time of the call and the nature of the call.* ■ *If you make recordings, make sure they are on tape so the tapes can go to police. Don't use a digital answering machine if the recording device cannot be transferred.* ■ *If you don't want to abruptly change your number, consider transitioning to a second phone line in your home and telling everyone to use that.* ■ *Consider a 30-day temporary change. By doing so, AT&T says, you can "possibly trick those who are making the calls" into thinking you have changed your number permanently.*

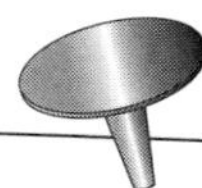

When annoyance calls come from harassers, do what I have done for 30 years. Introduce the caller to my make-believe friend, Detective Dominic LaRocca. You might have noticed that this book is dedicated to him: "You were always there when I needed you."

Detective LaRocca is always available to help you, 24/7.

I made him up. I picked the name because all three words sound tough: Detective…Dominic…LaRocca.

So when a caller who has called once or twice calls again, he hears me, in a much deeper voice, answer like this:

"Good evening, this is Detective Dominic LaRocca. How may I help you?"

Silence usually follows.

"Excuse me, whoever this is, please speak up now. This is an enforcement agency and I'm pretty busy."

Click.

Another way I do it is to answer as myself and say:

"Hello."

Silence.

"OK, Detective LaRocca start the trace NOW. I'll keep them on the line for as long as you need."

Click.

Years ago, I was interviewing a man for a story and asked him his name. He answered, Dominic LaRocca. I was speechless. All I could say was, "Oh, that's a common name."

He answered, "No, actually, it's not."

From: Ed and Betty
Sent: Thursday, January 10, 2008
To: Dave Lieber
Subject: Do Not Call List

We have a home phone listed on the "Do Not Call" list. In spite of this, we continue to receive calls from "Rate Reduction Center" offering us lower rates on credit cards. We ask the representative to be removed from their call list.

No luck. The caller ID shows "Unknown," so reporting them does no good.

Any suggestions?

From: Dave Lieber
Sent: Thursday, January 10, 2008
To: Ed and Betty
Subject: RE: Do Not Call List

Here's what I would say when they call:

"My lawyer has instructed me to inform you that I have asked repeatedly to be taken off your list because I am on the state and national Do Not Call lists. I am now taping this call and will tape all calls from you. We plan to file a lawsuit against you. We are also filing a complaint with the state attorney general. We traced your number through the phone company, so we now know who you are. I will not be hanging up because the longer you are on, the stronger is my legal case. Again, I repeat very clearly, please remove me from your list."

Then walk away from the phone, leaving it off the hook. Return later and hang it up.

More tricks that worked for me

Growing up in Manhattan during the high-crime era of the 1960s, I learned as a young boy to take extra security precautions. We had triple locks on our door and bars on some of the windows.

But when I left the city and moved elsewhere, there were times when I needed to come up with a few other tricks to help protect me.

Here are my favorite two, which you are welcome to "steal" any time!

Boots by the front door

I've heard it said you shouldn't put a sticker on your front door that states, "This house is protected by Smith & Wesson." Why? Because a robber will know there are guns in the house worth stealing. So what can you do to scare people off?

Well—and this works for people who live alone, especially women—I once found a well-worn pair of men's construction boots, size 13, encrusted with the scars of a construction job; tar, cement, scuff marks galore. Obviously, the guy who wore these boots was big and beefy. You definitely did not want to mess with him.

And what did I do with these boots?

I parked them permanently next to the welcome mat outside my front door.

Man in the window

Several times in my life, I have felt threatened enough by some situation that I knew the boots weren't going to do the trick. So here's what I did: I traced a silhouette of my body from the waist up on a sheet of newspaper and then spray-painted the sheet black.

Then I took this image of my upper body and pinned it to the blinds in the front window.

A lamp, placed on an automated timer, backlit the silhouette. If you passed by my house, it looked like a man in the window was watching.

The dude even scared me, and I put him there.

Let me talk you into something you don't need

"Need an oil change?" the man at the oil-change business asked me.

I told him it had been 8,000 miles since my last one.

"OK," he said. "Would you like a good synthetic oil like Pennzoil Platinum? Or we got Royal Purple. It's about $64, but you pay for two oil changes at once, you know. You can go 6,000 miles on it. It helps with gas by letting your engine run cooler. I mean, it's pretty good oil."

I asked how often the oil should be changed.

"We recommend 3,000 miles, because if you go beyond 3,000, you start getting sludge because conventional oil breaks down," the shop manager told me.

That pitch makes sense to many people who have been on that 3,000-mile schedule since they first got behind the wheel.

And some lube shops are only too happy to perpetuate the notion. My preferred oil changer gives me a window sticker urging me to come back every 3,000 miles.

But car manufacturers—and even the American Petroleum Institute, which has a vested interest in selling oil—say changing oil that often is unnecessary.

When I showed the manager that the owner's manual for my car recommended an oil change every 10,000 miles, he said, "We base it off API ratings—3,000 miles for the average, everyday driver."

He mentioned several more times that the API recommended an oil change every 3,000 miles. Indeed, he built his entire sales pitch around that recommendation.

Later, I called API, the main trade association for the oil and gas industry, and asked about that recommendation.

Kevin Ferrick, manager of API engine oil licensing, laughed and said:

"The 3,000-mile thing? I'm not really sure where it came from. Whatever that lube center is saying, if they're saying API has a recommended 3,000-mile interval, they're wrong. We don't have a recommended interval."

He recommended that drivers check their owner's manual.

For my car, 10,000 miles is appropriate for normal driving conditions.

For severe driving conditions, 5,000 miles might be more appropriate. Severe conditions include temperatures higher than 90 degrees, regular trips of less than five miles, excessive idling, or stop-and-go traffic.

General Motors spokesman Tom Henderson told me the average oil-change interval for a GM vehicle is 8,500 miles.

Henderson said changing the oil too often is wasteful, comparing it to discarding tires that aren't completely worn.

Before I left that lube center, the manager had asked me, "You sure you don't want your oil changed?"

No, thanks.

Follow the guidelines in your car's manual. ■ *If you drive in hot weather or do a lot of idling and stop-and-go driving in traffic, consider changing it more frequently, especially in the summer.* ■ *Check your oil regularly. If your car is burning oil, add more and consider more frequent oil changes. Ask a reputable mechanic why your engine is burning oil.* ■ *If you own a newer car that alerts you when an oil change is needed, heed the alert.* ■ *Don't always believe the salesman. Do a little research yourself so you know more about the subject than the salesman thinks you do.*

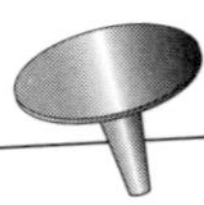

Give Lonnie Maxcy credit for chutzpah

Maxcy was angry that his many phone calls to the Fort Worth Water Department about his 98-year-old mother-in-law's high water bill went unanswered. So he pulled a move worthy of The Watchdog Nation.

He visited the water department carrying a bouquet of a dozen red roses.

An employee at the sign-in desk asked, "Who are the roses for?"

"It's for your deceased employee," he answered.

"Well, we didn't have an employee who died," the city worker answered.

Maxcy's comeback: "Obviously, you must be mistaken, because I've called here the last five days in a row and have left messages on your voice recorder, and I have not gotten a return call. So I just assumed she died. I came to pay my respects."

Turns out the employee had resigned and nobody was checking her voice mail.

His mother-in-law received a $146 refund.

Everybody's fantasy comes true

If you're like me, you've always dreamed of tracking down a scammer and confronting him or her.

Let me tell you: It feels good!

Marsha Ahrvide, a Fort Worth legal secretary, had a broken icemaker. She answered a newspaper ad placed by repairman Brian Littlefield. He told her he could fix it for $200.

Littlefield arrived at her home and replaced two parts. She paid him by check, and Littlefield told her to wait two hours for the icemaker to begin working. He gave her a slip of paper that he said represented a one-year warranty.

But the icemaker didn't work. Worse, it leaked so badly that ice froze into a large ball. She had to chip it out of the freezer.

She called to complain, but she couldn't reach him.

She tried to stop payment on the check, but he already cashed it.

When she finally reached him by phone, he promised to come back. But he never did. She called him again and this time he told her never to bother him again. So she bought another one elsewhere.

Meanwhile, it took me three weeks to find him. In the meantime, many of his former customers called and told me similar stories.

I tracked him down in East Texas. We talked on the phone. He acknowledged that he sometimes did not return customers' calls, but offered this reason:

"They are yelling and screaming and being hostile on the answering machine. I have a policy: If someone is hostile, I will not call him back."

"Why do you think they are hostile?" I asked.

"I'm not sure."

I think I know.

Call around and ask friends about repair people they have used. ■ Get bids, and if the bid is too low, it might be too good to be true. ■ Check whether a repair person has a storefront. ■ Check the BBB. ■ Trust your instincts.

Getting burned by a big brand name

If a company places its brand name on an appliance, does it have a responsibility to stand by it?

A few years ago, Holly West needed a water heater. She went to Lowe's Home Improvement Warehouse, looked at various Whirlpool brands and purchased one.

"That's the reason we bought it," she says. "It had the name Whirlpool on the side. And then it came back to bite us."

The water heater bit her the way a water heater can: It stopped working—more than once.

The problem was a safety sensor known as a thermocouple. The first time it broke, it was no big deal. The part was $10, and her husband knew how to fix it. Otherwise, it would have cost more than $100.

But then the thermocouple broke a second time. And then, a third time.

She decided to research the problem on the Internet. What she found surprised her.

Hundreds of owners of Whirlpool's Flame Lock and Flame Guard heaters, sold exclusively at Lowe's, were complaining about the same problem.

Some sample comments:

John of New York: "I have since replaced the thermocouple five times, at my cost. ... The last time I replaced the thermocouple was three months ago. Guess what? The thing went south again!"

John of Louisiana: "Installed new water heater and had to change thermocouple three times in the first six months. Also, just replaced thermocouple on sister-in-law's 1-year-old Whirlpool water heater four times, and it's out again."

West contacted Whirlpool and Lowe's but wasn't satisfied with their response. "I'm pretty upset because nobody wanted to admit it was faulty," she told me.

After she contacted me, I typed these words into an Internet search engine:"

"Whirlpool water heater and class action lawsuit"

It got a quick hit.

A class-action lawsuit settlement about this very problem would reimburse a portion of the replacement costs to all affected Whirlpool water heater owners who purchased from Lowe's from 2000 to 2006.

As explained at www.waterheatersettlement.com, owners of Flame Lock and Flame Guard water heaters will be eligible for replacement thermocouples and other parts.

Owners who gave up after three thermocouple failures and purchased another brand of water heater are eligible for $150.

What responsibility does Whirlpool accept for this pervasive flaw?

Not much.

The water heaters, a Whirlpool spokeswoman told me, are "manufactured by American Water Heater and licensed and sold under the Whirlpool brand name to Lowe's. Although Whirlpool was named in the lawsuit, Whirlpool did not manufacture the water heater nor any of its components."

American Water Heater defended Whirlpool and Lowe's in the lawsuit. The company contended that the product was defect-free. Still, the company agreed to settle the litigation while disclaiming any liability.

As a claimant in the lawsuit, West is eligible for $30.

That covers the three thermocouples, but not the labor.

"That's very disappointing," she said. "It sounds like they are getting out pretty good."

She's right.

Don't assume a brand name represents the same excellence in quality that it did a decade ago. ■ Before making any major purchase, note the product name, manufacturer and model number and type it into an Internet search engine followed by the word "complaint." See what comes up. ■ Read product reviews on the Internet before buying. ■ Search blogs and groups, too, to find out if customers are chatting about recurring problems. ■ When you have a problem, always check if it is part of a class-action lawsuit.

TV sets are better, but hassle is greater

In olden days when you bought a television set, you plunked down $200 or so and got a TV that lasted for a decade.

Today's TV sets are better (high-definition), bigger (they can fill an entire wall) and, of course, costlier. Bigger TVs, bigger problems.

People complain a lot about their TVs these days. I hear from folks who are upset about both the buying process and the repair process.

Larry Collier shopped for an HDTV for months. He watched prices drop from $4,000 to under $3,000. At a Best Buy store, he found what he was looking for—a 46-inch beauty with hidden bottom speakers and a 10-bit processor offering 12.8 billion colors. (I didn't know there were that many colors!)

Price: $2,799.99.

The best part was the we-can't-be-beat promise. A Best Buy salesman offered him a 60-day "HDTV Price Guarantee." If he found the set at a lower advertised price from a local competitor within two months, the store would match the price with a refund and pay an additional 10 percent difference.

He bought it. Less than a month later, he saw the price for the set drop lower at a competitor's store. He went to Best Buy, but sales clerks there told him the store was in a neighboring city, about 20 miles away, and not local enough.

He left the store, then returned a few days later to plead his case again. Same reply.

Fuming, he contacted me. I told him to forget the store and call Best Buy's customer service at corporate headquarters.

Simple enough. He followed my suggestion and got a $444 refund. A Best Buy spokesman later apologized.

Then there's the repair side of the equation. Although repair rates are very low for LCD and plasma screens, according to *Consumer Reports*, about 15 percent of TV owners in a *CR* survey found that they had serious problems getting their sets repaired under warranty. Seems like most of those 15 percent have contacted me.

Clement Punzalan made a mistake when he failed to buy an extended warranty for his 42-inch Samsung HDTV. He figured that the Samsung name is so valued that the set would hold up. But he forgot that TV sets seems to know when a warranty is about to expire. They break days or weeks after the expiration date.

Since the original warranty had just expired, he tried to contact Samsung for help. The company didn't bother to answer him for two months. He tried again, and finally was told tough luck, pal.

I had no better luck going to bat for him. Samsung didn't return my calls either.

Punzalan came up with a great way to shop to avoid these situations: "Customers should not only research a price but also try to call the manufacturer's customer service number and determine if the response is good," he says. "Determine if you get bounced from one voice machine to another or if it takes one hour before you get connected to a person.

"If you don't get satisfaction before you purchase a product, it is very unlikely you will get it after the purchase."

I love his advice. It's sad that it has come to this, but it has.

Before purchasing a product, do an Internet search for complaints about the product from customers. See if you can detect a pattern that might affect your planned purchase. ■ *Call the customer service number for the product and test whether you get bounced around a voice-mail system and how long it takes to reach a human who could solve a problem. Check whether you are allowed to speak to a supervisor.* ■ *Before you buy, check prices on the store's Web site. Print the results and take them with you. Sometimes the Web price is cheaper than the store price.* ■ *Get details for price-matching offers in writing. Constantly check prices in ads after you buy.* ■ *Some stores offer extended warranties for free. Ask a salesperson about it.* ■ *Buy the set using a premium credit card that offers its own extended warranty.* ■ *Keep original store receipts, credit card receipts and the actual warranty card.*

Banks don't give out toasters anymore

Carolyn Russell was low on two life essentials—money in her checking account and gasoline in her car. She called Compass Bank to find out how much was available in her checking account.

The answer? $2.32.

So she went out and bought $2.32 worth of gas, hoping it would carry her until her next disability check arrived in the mail.

But eight days later, she received a notice from the bank: Her account was overdrawn, and she was required to pay $36 to cover the insufficient funds. An additional penalty of $6 a day would be assessed beginning after the first week.

The amount of her overdraft?

Two cents.

She believed that she must have made a mistake—even though she spent the exact amount the bank told her was available. So she called 1-800-COMPASS, as directed on the notice.

A customer service representative told her that the bank's computer system was down. The best thing to do, the representative said, was visit an area bank branch and pay the $36.

So the next day, she borrowed $36 from a friend and drove to a Compass Bank. But when she tried to pay at the teller window, she recalls, she was told that her bill—because of penalties—had grown to more than $70.

She returned home and visited the bank branch, where she had opened her account five years before, hoping to speak to the manager.

"He was busy with another client," she recalls. A teller told her that she would take Russell's name and number and ask a supervisor to call.

"But I never got the call," she says.

I learned about her problem and decided to put in my two cents' worth. By then, her penalties were more than $100.

Russell wasn't shirking her responsibility: "I expected them to at least let me pay the $36…but they didn't," she says.

The way I viewed it, there were several breakdowns. And when I shared my analysis with Compass Bank spokesman Tim Deighton, based at headquarters in Birmingham, Ala., he did not disagree.

Here they are:

1) Russell says she spent the exact amount the bank said she had available.

2) The notice of insufficient funds took a week to arrive in the mail. Deighton says the bank's policy is to notify customers quickly by telephone to avoid escalating penalties. Russell says she never got a call.

3) When she called the bank's toll-free number and was told that the computer system was down, nobody offered to take her name and number and call her back.

4) She was told that she owed $36, but when she came prepared to pay, she learned that the amount was more.

5) When she left her name and number for the bank manager to call her back, no one did.

"There's a communication breakdown somewhere between her and the branch," Deighton told me. "Considering her situation, I'm surprised that we didn't waive the fees."

He said a longtime customer on a limited income with such a small overdraft should have been sent to the bank's Customer Care Unit. That never happened either.

The bank credited Russell's account.

Russell could have returned to the bank and demanded a sit-down with the manager. But not everyone is an aggressive member of The Watchdog Nation. Sorry, but if you aren't, these uncaring souls will run all over you!

Ask for a sit-down with higher-ups. ■ If you don't get it, complain to corporate headquarters. ■ If that still doesn't work, switch banks. There's a lot of competition. Take advantage of it. ■ Find out from your bank who regulates the bank. A state banking department? A federal agency? File a complaint. ■ If you can't find out from the bank, contact the Federal Deposit Insurance Corporation at 1-877-ASK-FDIC or visit www.FDIC.gov and ask for information about your bank's regulators.

Watchdog Nation Core Principle #5:

Apply the pressure point and squeeze

You've tried everything. You looked up the company before you bought from it but still got burned. You made the reps accountable. You taped your calls. You found the company's point of vulnerability. You asked a bunch of questions.

Nothing worked.

Now it's time for the nuclear option. There's no turning back.

Everybody, or almost everybody, answers to a higher power. No, I'm not turning religious on you (although there should be a page in this book that says simply, "When all else fails, pray!").

The higher power is an auditor, regulator, certifier, inspector, licensor, inspector or permit issuer who lords over your nemesis. Everybody is scared of somebody.

In most cases, there is a state licensor or a federal regulator—or both.

Once you find out who and what that pressure point is, you squeeze. You can usually get some unexpected results.

The woman who contacted me about her family's heirloom furniture being damaged by a mover and the mover wouldn't return her calls? No sweat.

We found out who regulated movers in her state and filed a complaint with that state agency. Turns out the state agency offers free mediation. Who knew?

The woman whose home warranty company refused to cover a repair on a refrigerator? No problem. We asked the magic search engine box this question: "Who regulates home warranty companies?"

We learned that the state real estate commission audits the financial books of each home warranty company every two years and then reissues a license.

Suddenly the woman was no longer a nagging complainer at company headquarters. Her complaint was mailed on official letterhead to the company from the state in which she lived. And suddenly, she had a number that reflected her official complaint. She wasn't that annoying Mrs. Jones who kept bugging the home office. Now she was 2010-34353A. That's clout.

Within a week a company may call and say, "Uh, there's been a misunderstanding. If we come by and fix the part for free, will you sign a letter dropping your complaint against us with the state? Our license is up for renewal."

Your best answer: "I'll think about it."

My favorite example of how to make an unyielding institution cry "Uncle!" involves Amanda Godawski, a young woman who thought she transferred money into her checking account using her home computer. But the transfer didn't go through, and Compass Bank charged her $579 in overdraft fees and $7-per-day charges.

She fought the bank, stopped using the account and asked to close it. But the bank wouldn't let her.

When the U.S. Treasury direct-deposited her federal income tax refund and then her stimulus check into the account, Compass Bank confiscated the money and applied it to the charges.

Along with her father, Ted, they contacted elected officials and others. When I inquired, the bank flatly told me it was Godawski's error.

Amanda's dad sent a local congressman a letter about the matter. U.S. Rep. Kenny Marchant, R-Texas, sits on the House Financial Services Committee, which, um, happens to write laws that regulate bank such as Compass. Oopsie.

The congressman contacted the bank: "I just asked if they would consider refunding the fees," he recalled.

"The bank should have closed her account when it became obvious that she lost control of it," the congressman said. "It would have saved them and her a lot of grief."

After the congressman's call, Compass wrote Godawski a letter stating that a search of its computer system's raw data showed that she had logged on and tried to make a transfer, but it didn't go through. Denying any error, the bank decided to refund $465 anyway, without mentioning the remaining $114. A check was enclosed.

The six-page letter, with repeated denials of wrongdoing and detailed explanations of bank policies, offers far greater detail than any of the bank's previous communications with her. A notation at the bottom shows a copy was sent to the congressman.

A bank spokesman told me that the congressman's inquiry had no effect on the bank's change of heart. "It's not because the congressman called," he said. "We try and work with our customers, OK?"

OK.

Rep. Marchant says, "Hopefully, the bank will change its policy."

Ted Godawski says, "No one is going to steal money from my daughter."

Federal regulators for banks and other lending regulations include: FDIC, Federal Reserve System, Office of the Comptroller of the Currency and the National Credit Union Administration. ■ Check also with your state banking department. ■ The newest player on the regulatory block is the U.S. Consumer Financial Protection Bureau, which opened for business in 2011. Its website – consumerfinance.gov – is an impoprtant place to start when having problems with any financial institution. Phone 202-435-7000.

THE STRATEGY

Squeeze 'em where it hurts!

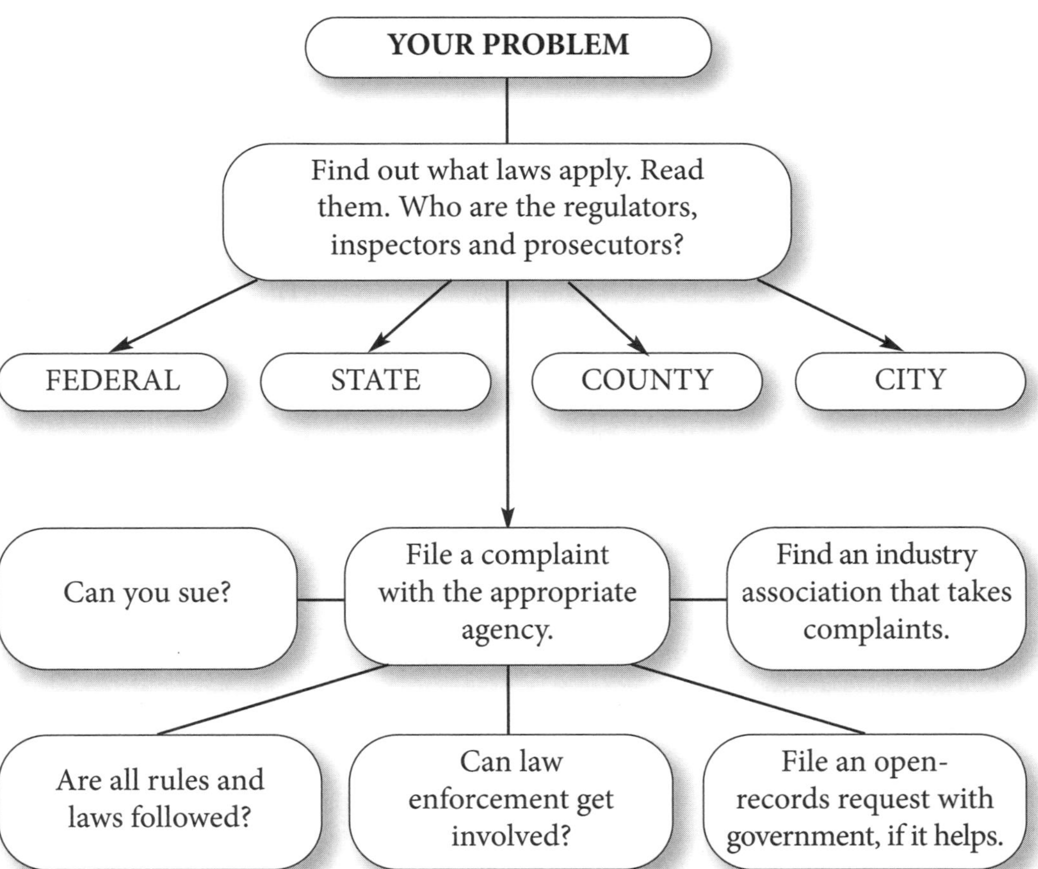

YOUR PROBLEM
Find out what laws apply. Read them. Who are the regulators, inspectors and prosecutors?
FEDERAL
STATE
COUNTY
CITY
Can you sue?
File a complaint with the appropriate agency.
Find an industry association that takes complaints.
Are all rules and laws followed?
Can law enforcement get involved?
File an open-records request with government, if it helps.

The check's in the mail. Not always a good thing.

Be wary when you get unexpected money in the mail, even if it's a cashier's check.

Devona Jackson was quite surprised when a bank cashier's check for $4,880 made out to her arrived in December. Who doesn't want extra cash before the holidays?

The accompanying letter explained that the sender was "a secret customer service employment firm that specializes in the assisting of corporations on how to improve customer service to their clientele."

The letter offered to hire Jackson to work as a mystery shopper and promised that "all fees have been waived."

The letter looked good, and the attached form looked even better. Logos for big-name companies such as McDonald's, Wal-Mart, FedEx and Burger King were placed above the heading "Customer Service Evaluation Tool" at the top.

Jackson read the form and understood that she was supposed to shop at stores and businesses and then grade sales representatives for their dress, courtesy, manner and efficiency. All she had to do was cash the $4,880 cashier's check, spend $50 at Wal-Mart, $40 at The Gap, keep $500 for herself, and make wire transfers of $2,700 by Western Union and $1,400 by MoneyGram to Canada. The rest went to associated fees.

Jackson, a hospital office assistant, was suspicious. She contacted me.

I took a copy of the check and called the phone number for the issuing bank: United Republic Bank of Omaha. There was a quick busy signal—not a good sign. Then I looked up the actual phone number of the bank, and it was different. I called the bank in Nebraska.

Venita Spier, the bank's chief operations officer, told me that the check was part of a scam that had prompted several hundred people to call her bank asking about the legitimacy of the checks.

Several people had fallen for the scam, she said. They cashed the checks and then, days later, found out that the business wasn't legitimate.

They owed their banks $4,880. The money wired via Western Union and MoneyGram went to

Canada, she said, where the scammers collected big-time.

"We have contacted local enforcement, the FBI, the regulatory agencies and the United States Postal Service," Spier told me.

There are legitimate mystery-shopping businesses. Typically, a shopper is reimbursed and allowed to keep the product they bought in return for a completed customer service report.

In the past, cashier's checks were seen as solid, almost equivalent to cash, and a surefire way to quickly transfer money. But these checks are fake.

"With today's technology, it's considerably easier to make a forged check, even a cashier's check," a spokesman for the Federal Deposit Insurance Corporation says. "You can put check-writing software on your home computer, and you can be in business. Now it's a couple of clicks of a mouse, and you have a check."

According to the Federal Trade Commission, here's how this scam works:

You cash the check, do the shopping and wire off the rest of the money. A few days later, you get a call from your bank that the check is no good. If Jackson had gone through with it, she would have owed her bank $4,880.

Legitimate companies are registered with the Mystery Shopping Providers Association. Its Web site (www.mysteryshop.org) states that legitimate companies never promise large sums of fast cash or require fees.

If somebody you don't know gives you a check, wait until the full amount is deposited in your bank account before spending the money. Don't mistake the end of a hold period as the final test of a check's legitimacy.

"A lot of times, holds are lifted on a check before a check actually clears the system," the FDIC spokesman says. "So it's two separate things. Banks hold checks three to five days before the money becomes available, but that doesn't mean the check has cleared the system."

Be especially wary of companies that advertise in a newspaper's help wanted section or by e-mail.

- *Legitimate companies don't sell certification to customers or guarantee a job as a mystery shopper.*
- *If you are asked to cash a check to participate, don't do it.*

Hunt for what you're owed in life insurance

As a 21-year-old working at the Fort Worth bomber plant in 1953, Roberta Welch decided to buy a $500 life insurance policy on her husband, figuring it might be needed for burial expenses someday.

She bought the policy from Rio Grande National Life Insurance Co. of Dallas, owned by Robert Baxter, who had a Texas-size ego. In a *Time* magazine story in the late 1940s about the nation's economy, he was quoted as saying, "This is a great world and the U.S. is the greatest country in the world—and Texas is the greatest state in the U.S. and Dallas is the greatest city in Texas and the Rio Grande is the greatest insurance company in Dallas."

Every week for 20 years, someone from Rio Grande, and then its successor, Kentucky Central Life, made the rounds of the neighborhood and picked up Welch's weekly insurance premium payment—all of 32 cents.

By 1973, the policy was paid off. Welch put the paperwork away, and when her husband died 12 years later, she decided to hold off on cashing in the policy.

Years passed, and she lost track of the policy. Then, two years ago, she found it and decided to collect. She tried to call Rio Grande and Kentucky Central Life but both had gone out of business (KCL went insolvent in Kentucky in the mid-1990s).

She contacted Lincoln Financial Group, a company that she thought had inherited her policy, but they couldn't find it.

Welch, who is 76, thought it was a lost cause. Then she contacted me.

It turns out that millions of dollars' worth of life insurance policies are never cashed because relatives don't know about them or policyholders forget about them or lose the papers.

Sometimes a company changes hands so many times that it takes a little detective work to track the policy down.

That's what happened here. Welch's Rio Grande policy finally ended up at Reliable Life Insurance in 1991.

Welch, who has lived at the same address in Hurst for decades, said she never received notices about her policy's status. When she tried to locate the company last year, her request for information to Lincoln Financial was answered with a request for more information and this curt reply: "We were unable to identify a policy number that it should be applied to."

When I contacted Lincoln Financial, the company took a second look, and this time it found a link to her policy at Reliable Insurance.

Lincoln officials contacted Reliable and arranged for Welch to file the proper paperwork to retrieve her $500—plus interest.

"You were my last chance," she told me.

But that's not true. It may take some digging and patience, but a paid-up policy must be covered, even if the originating company is no longer in business.

State insurance officials can often help consumers track down the information. Kelvin Beck, senior insurance specialist for the Texas Insurance Department's consumer protection division, helps consumers locate lost policies. He says Welch's story is not that unusual.

"You have to follow each path to a current or active company," Beck says. "It's basically like [tracing] genealogy."

Start with your state's department of insurance. Officials there will help you trace. ■ *Search your family's old records for more information, ask relatives, seek out the family insurance agent.* ■ *For $75, MIB checks some insurance information that may help you find a lost policy. Records go back to 1995. Call 1-781-751-6000 or visit www.policylocator.com. MIB reports a 30 percent success rate.* ■ *Check with your state's unclaimed property fund.* ■ *Check other databases such as www.missingmoney.org, www.nupn.com and www.unclaimed.org.* ■ *Talk to family members about policies and keep all insurance documents together.*

The revolution has begun

A few years ago, it would have been impossible to launch and sustain The Watchdog Nation.

Now, we have more power than ever before—but many of us aren't quite yet sure how to use it against those who try to take advantage of us.

So far in this guidebook, I've shown how you can research any situation and learn how to solve your problems because of experiences and details already learned by others. You start by going to a search engine and typing in your question.

When I joined the newspaper business 30 years ago, if I wanted to learn something, I usually had to take a few hours at the library or go through stacks of public records.

Now I can get the same answer to my question in seconds. I can do more, quicker. And so can you.

If you have a problem that you can't solve, try to find a Web site where the problem is discussed and post your situation.

Remember, that posting supposedly sticks around for eternity. People researching the same problem later will come across your note. The Internet is a global bulletin board on any subject. And it comes with instant connectivity and immediately links to searchable databases. This is one of the most amazing developments, I dare say, in the history of the human race.

And now we can use this amazing gift to burn a hole right through those who try to burn us.

Jeff Jarvis is a journalism professor at City University of New York, not exactly a bully pulpit to change the world. But Jarvis also runs www.buzzmachine.com. And he uses that blog to post items about corporate America that get reclusive executives to smack their foreheads in frustration.

Here's how Jarvis discovered his new-found power:

"In June 2005, I unwittingly unleashed a blog storm around [Dell Computer]. Terminally frustrated with a lemony laptop and torturous service, I vented steam on my blog, Buzzmachine.com, under the headline: 'Dell sucks.' "

Thousands of others posted to his blog, too, with comments that could be summarized as "Me, too."

Both Jarvis and Dell now say this development helped change the internal culture of Dell.

New initiatives were created and service measurements showed higher satisfaction rates.

Bob Garfield, a media critic and radio host, learned the same lesson when, frustrated with his cable telephone service, he created a Web site called ComcastMustDie.com.

Thousands of postings followed. Soon after, Comcast officials began trying to contact the posters to fix their problems. As Garfield points out, executives were using ComcastMustDie to work feverishly to solve complaints and get positive posts in return. I do believe this is the future.

"This is all made possible by the digital revolution, by the web of broadband that connects us all," Garfield told ABC's *Nightline*. "They strung the very cable that I now wrap around their neck. … The beauty of the digital age is you don't have to take it any more. You are no longer just screaming into the dark."

He added, "It's the beginning. The genie, sorry to use the cliché, is out of the bottle, and it's never going to get put back in."

Note: As an example of the power of the World Wide Web, I wanted to check Bob Garfield's quotes for accuracy. So I typed "Bob Garfield and Nightline" into a search engine and—voila—actual video of his ABC interview popped up on www.YouTube.com. It's an information miracle. Use it to its full advantage.

Computer Forum
DELL BITES!

Social Media changes company-customer relationship

Twitter. Hate it or love it, but its effect on human communication is undeniable. For the first time in recorded history, anyone can "broadcast" a thought, a quote, a referral or an ad, and it can come in text, photo or video format. And for free!

Your thoughts, around the world, to anyone who wants them. Instantaneously.

It's the Tower of Babel.

Companies now monitor Twitter on a second-by-second basis. Any negative mention and someone from that company likely will "Direct Message" you offering help. Anything to stop the bad news about the company from being shouted from the Tower of Babel.

I ran a little experiment to see if my power changed any from that of a newspaper columnist to that of a Twitterer. The Twitter response was more poignant than I imagined. Here's what happened:

Attention Mattress Giant: If you knew the bed was bad, why did you sell it to me?

The trend that I hate the most, really hate, is that it takes most service personnel two times, at least, to get things right. We used to live in a nation where almost everybody got things right the first time.

Now you hire somebody to do something, and most likely they will have to come back because they didn't get it right the first time.

For example, the security alarm guy from ADT visited Watchdog Nation HQ to help protect our top-secret investigative files.

He was back again the next day. He forgot to alarm the back door.

The new brakes that were put on Watchdog Nation's Batmobile? We had to return and get them replaced after 24 hours. Defective parts.

But the one that stands out among second chances is the one involving Mattress Giant.

We bought a new bed. Of course, when they delivered it, they forgot to bring the bed frame.

No problem. I went to the store and picked it up. Yeah, second chances. I expect the incompetence.

By the second night, however, the box springs were so creaky we couldn't stand it. Every move on that bed sounded like a stack of plates crashing to the floor. LOUD. CRASH. WAKE UP.

We returned to the store, and the woman at the counter apologized. She told us there might be a $59 exchange fee.

I started reading their statement of principles hanging on the store wall. Standing behind their service. Quality. Blah blah blah.

She got the fee waived.

Then I asked her how come the box springs made so much noise.

She explained it was part of "a bad batch" that had come from the bed factory.

I asked, "If you knew the batch was bad, why did you sell it to me?"

She replied, "Well, some of the bad ones got mixed in with the rest."

EXCUSE ME?!

Have you ever heard of barcodes? Inventory control? Finding the bad ones in the lot AND PULLING THEM OFF THE SHELVES?

I got another box springs, but the more I thought about it, the angrier I got. I believe Mattress Giant knowingly sold me a bad bed. How else to explain that they knew the batch was bad but sold it anyway?

I called Graeme Gordon, the vice president of marketing and advertising for Mattress Giant (listed on the company Web site as the PR contact), to discuss this with him. He didn't call back, at least not right away.

An employee at the International Bedding Corp. factory told me she wasn't aware of any bad box springs, but if there was a bad lot, "We sell it to Mattress Giant, and if they have an issue, they'll talk to our production manager. If you have a problem, talk to Mattress Giant."

I posted the above information on WatchdogNation.com/blog, Twitter @DaveLieber and Dave Lieber's Watchdog Nation on Facebook.

Within minutes after the Twitter post, a Mattress Giant representative sent me a direct message via Twitter. A few minutes later, Gordon, who at first didn't call back, called to respond to the post. The vice president then apologized.

"We're in the middle of a meeting and I wanted to step out to let you know that I know what was going on," he said.

"This comes down to someone at the store level who unfortunately isn't aware of what is going on....

"We knew something wasn't right was because we saw returns jump from 1 to 5 percent... There was a flaw in the design.

"The manufacturer told us they were completely redesigning the box springs. So there's no excuse for getting it mixed in.

"I'm not one to give excuses, and honestly, there's no reason that should have happened....

"If anyone calls and says they've got the same problem, I'll bring them one tomorrow. I'll give them a pillow, whatever it takes to get the problem solved. ... I'm going to ask you: Can I send you a pillow to make up for this?"

I said, "Thank you for the gesture, but I'm not in this for the free gifts."

That taught me the power of Twitter. It got their attention. Fast.

*Follow @DaveLieber on Twitter. * Like facebook.com/watchdognation. * Visit www.Facebook.com/dave.lieber. * Visit www.WatchdogNation.com/blog for the latest. * Watch videos at www.YouTube.com/WatchdogNation.*

Run your own campaign

What if you have a problem, for example, with XYZ Vacuum Cleaner Co.? How do you get the company to fix your problem?

Let's brainstorm a few ideas:

1) First, try the customer service hotline. Then ask for a supervisor. Then ask for the supervisor's supervisor.

2) Research the corporate officials. Find their e-mail addresses or send them letters.

3) Complain to the Better Business Bureau.

4) Complain to your state attorney general's consumer protection division.

5) Find out if there is a Vacuum Dealers Association in your state and file a complaint.

6) Tell all your friends what happened in a brief e-mail. Copy it to XYZ officials if you know their addresses. Don't use derogatory or libelous language. Don't say that the company is crooked. Just state your problem.

7) Find Web sites where others who have had problems with XYZ posted their complaints.

8) Print a bumper sticker (search "print bumper sticker" on an Internet search engine to find a company that will do this) and place it on your car.

9) Contact the management of the store where you bought the vacuum cleaner.

10) Place a video about your problem on YouTube.com.

11) In general, do everything you can to get attention so that XYZ notices you and realizes that you are such a pain that it's easier to solve your problem than allow your campaign, which could cost them sales, to continue.

Make a difference by getting involved

If you want to fight back against a particular industry or company that has mistreated you, here's how you can make a difference.

Find a citizens watchdog group that tries to raise public awareness about problems in that industry. These groups, typically, also lobby state and federal lawmakers to change laws regulating the industry so they are more favorable to consumers.

Most of these organizations have a national headquarters and then state and even local chapters.

These groups would love for you to volunteer and help them achieve their pro-consumer goals.

Many of these lobbyists operate on shoestring budgets and don't have much money for staff. Often, they have just a few paid officials and the remaining members are volunteers.

They go up against lobbying groups that are funded by the industries they serve. These groups often give tremendous amounts of money in campaign donations to lawmakers who write the laws that regulate their industry.

The only counterbalance to big money/backroom power plays are these citizen action groups. Your work with them can make a big difference.

*Use an Internet search engine to find a group that is dedicated to fighting a problem that interests you. Type in words like "citizens group" or "consumer rights" and the name of the company or industry involved. * Familiarize yourself with the work of the U.S. Consumer Financial Protection Bureau at consumerfinance.gov.*

Best strategy advice for The Watchdog Nation

No surprise that I learned a basic component of Watchdog Nation strategy from a former Green Beret.

Now a firefighter, Jeff Natterer battled a towing company that he said improperly towed his car from a parking lot.

As someone who jumped out of airplanes and led missions as a captain in the Green Berets, he says, "I see the world in black and white."

A short man with burning eyes that reflect his good-guy-versus-bad-guy outlook, Natterer's saga began when he discovered his blue pickup missing from the lot. At first, he thought the pickup was stolen. He called police dispatch and learned that a tow truck operator had grabbed the vehicle for improperly parking in a private lot.

Thinking wisely, Natterer and his wife took out a camera and snapped 24 photographs of the parking lot from various angles. His shots included several of the required "NO PARKING" signs. Photos showed that the signs were faded and unreadable.

Then the Special Forces captain launched his latest battle. What's telling, though, is the way he fought back—using a computer, small-claims court and open-records requests. It's a winning Watchdog Nation strategy that anyone can follow.

Natterer sat at his computer and typed "Texas law and transportation code" into an Internet search engine. He quickly found a Texas law that protects vehicle owners from improper towing.

"They towed the vehicle without cause," Natterer said. "It's really like stealing a vehicle. They lacked the authority to remove the vehicle."

His worldview kicked in: "In this case, they've come out of the gray area and into the black area."

He found out who regulates towing and what the law allows for consumers who believe they are victimized.

As the law allowed, he sued the towing company in small-claims court. Within weeks, his case was called. With his photographs and his understanding of the law, Natterer won the case: "Probable cause did not exist for towing," court record shows.

The court ordered the towing company to refund Natterer's money.

Then he filed an open-records request with the police department to examine police towing records.

From his reading of the state towing law, he learned that permanent signs must be posted at each entrance, giving towing rules, a contact phone number and other information. The signs must be large and easy to read.

A towing company must have a written agreement with a property owner before towing someone's vehicle off that property. (None existed here.)

And he found another loophole—towing companies must comply with state registration requirements, too.

See all these steps that must be followed by businesses? If any one of these steps is not followed, that leaves an opening for the "victim" to fight back. ~

Find the law that applies to your situation. Read it looking for ways that can help you overcome your problem. ■ The law will tell you what state agency regulates the industry. Check with the agency and ask if the company involved has complied with all state requirements. Is it licensed? Did it pay its taxes? Are its insurance and registration information current? ■ Find the state or national association that covers that particular industry. Often, the association will take complaints and try to handle them internally before the government gets involved. ■ File an open-records request with the government to find out all you can about the company. ■ Build your case by taking photographs and video.

Bypass bad customer service by seeking help in forums

Here's a way to avoid bad customer service. Find the Internet "forums" in which customers can ask questions. Sometimes, you'll get a volunteer such as Justin McMurry. He cares. Why? Because he remembers how he was treated when he called Verizon customer service to complain about his FiOS television service.

"I was getting a little testy," he told me. "I asked for his employee number. All I heard was click."

McMurry, a retired IBM systems engineer, began answering questions on Verizon's online community forum, a Web site where Verizon customers can get help with TV, Internet or telephone service problems.

He's so good at it that he is called a top-ranked "Community Leader" based on the many kudos he has received from those he has helped at the site. That's all he gets. See, McMurry does it for free. He's not a Verizon employee. Yet the 68-year-old spends up to 20 hours a week researching and answering questions.

Using volunteers to supplement a company's technical support is a growing trend because it saves companies from having to pay staff to handle phone calls and make service visits.

A Verizon spokesman said the volunteer service is "a small slice" of the company's customer service program. "Super-users" such as McMurry do not have access to customers' personal accounts, but they can answer technical questions. Customers can still contact Verizon directly.

McMurry calls Verizon's in-house customer service "horrid." He says, "Companies just don't care anymore. Apparently, it's all about the almighty dollar."

But not for these volunteers. So you should try to find them. · ~

*Find forums by asking a search engine for "customer forums for [name of product]." * McMurry volunteers at forums.verizon.com/vrzn. * Visit highdefforum.com for high-definition tech problems. Visit dslreports.com for forums on a variety of high-tech subjects.*

So sue me! OK, I will.

Small-claims court is fun! You have a lot more power to fight back than you know.

I had one of my best days when I put on my lawyerly pinstriped suit and carried my finest leather briefcase into small claims to sue my homebuilder over a faulty air conditioning system.

I brought copies of all relevant paperwork, an expert witness and a strategy designed to get back some of the money I lost trying to solve the problem, including excess and unnecessary payments to the electric company for an inefficient system.

The homebuilder sent a Dallas lawyer who was wearing a nicer suit than mine. His briefcase was better, too. Plus, he carried a smug look on his face.

But I had seen enough episodes of *Perry Mason* to believe that I knew what I was doing.

I had a field day punching away at the testimony of the other side's star witness during my cross-examination and proving that the builder hadn't complied with the building code. What fun!

But there was one moment of great danger when the Dallas lawyer stood to move that my case be dismissed. The lawyer read aloud 14 subclauses of the law, and he convinced even me that I had no case. I didn't know what to do.

"Do you have an answer to that, Mr. Lieber?" the judge asked.

It was the longest minute of my life as I grabbed a copy of the law and began scanning for a loophole. Finally, I looked at the 15th subclause—which the lawyer had not read aloud. I still don't know what it means, but I stood and read it aloud: *The inspection and repair provisions of this chapter are in addition to any rights of inspection and settlement provided by common law by another statute.*

Even if I didn't understand it, the judge did because he didn't dismiss my case. I'll never forget the scowl that crossed the Dallas lawyer's face.

The judge awarded me court costs plus $800 plus to cover excessive utility bills. He said he would have given me more, but I made the mistake of not asking for more. Darn!

Yet it wasn't only about money. What matters is the great concept that you don't need a lawyer to stand up for your rights and win. The system can work. But only if you're willing to use it.

Beware of hospital-acquired infections

Your mother enters the hospital for knee-replacement surgery. Two weeks later, she's readmitted, but this time she has to be hooked up to a ventilator because a hospital-acquired infection, resistant to antibiotics, has entered her bloodstream. She could die.

Your best friend has successful cancer surgery. But while recovering, he catches a "superbug" when drug-resistant bacteria enter his body through a urinary catheter. He has a high fever and redness near the incisions. When his lungs shut down, he deteriorates quickly and goes on a ventilator. He spends weeks in the hospital with the cost ballooning.

An estimated 2 million Americans annually get one of a variety of drug-resistant infections, leading to about 90,000 deaths, the federal Centers for Disease Control and Prevention estimate.

Of those afflicted, 87 percent catch the infection at a healthcare facility, the CDC says.

But those are only estimates. Because there is no nationwide or even state-by-state database, nobody knows for sure how many people are infected, where they got infected and which healthcare facilities have the worst infection rates.

"There's a lot of denial among hospital administrations" about hospital infection rates, said a superbug expert, Dr. Jon Lloyd.

Ideally, your mother or your friend could shop around before surgery for hospitals with low infection rates, maybe by visiting a Web site with hospital statistics.

But in most states, consumers do not have access to that vital information. Why? It's not even collected. It's not collected nationally either.

Amazing. In Texas, for example, legislators voted to create a state Infection Reporting System. But lawmakers didn't provide any money for it. So Texas hospitals are still not required to keep statistics or report them to the state.

Texas lawmakers passed another infections-related bill that would create a one-year pilot program in three urban areas to collect information about one of the best-known infections—*methicillin-resistant Staphylococcus aureus*, a superbug that can resist antibiotics.

MRSA causes about 19,000 deaths a year nationwide.

Hospital-acquired infections are easily spread among healthcare workers and from patient to patient by hands, equipment and clothing. Severe ones resist regular treatment by antibiotics.

Medical experts say that public reporting is an important step toward lowering infection rates.

"It may make some people really sit up, take notice and take the steps they should be taking to get rid of it," said Dr. David Jefferson, environmental health manager at Tarrant County Public Health in Texas.

Lisa McGiffert of Consumers Union in Austin runs a national campaign to get states to require infection-rate reporting. The campaign's Web site—StopHospitalInfections.org—displays news reports about hospital infections nationwide.

"We know there's a great deal hospitals can do to prevent these infections, but they're not doing them," McGiffert said.

"We believe that publicly reporting each hospital's infection rate will motivate hospitals to take up these techniques, improve the care at their hospital and prevent infections."

The problem, McGiffert and other health experts say, is that aside from the danger of patients dying, the added costs of treating infections strain an already overburdened healthcare system.

Public reporting is the first step, they say, to ending the problem and saving lives.

Contact your state and federal lawmakers and demand they tighten reporting requirements for hospital-acquired infections. You must provide a counterbalance to powerful hospital lobbyists who spend hundreds of thousands of dollars. ▪ *If you or a family member is a patient in a healthcare facility, be vigilant in asking hospital workers—doctors, nurses and others—to wash their hands before treating you.* ▪ *Be especially careful of any open sores and wounds. Make sure they are properly covered.* ▪ *Wash your hands frequently.*

More Principles of The Watchdog Nation

1) Bring order to your Watchdog Nation world. Use files to hold all receipts, warranties and contracts for purchases. Keep a separate file for copies of correspondence related to any product rebates you are owed. As the guys in my old neighborhood used to say, "Make dem guys pay what they owes ya!"

2) Complain to your state attorney general when you feel victimized. The AG's office may already be investigating the source of your complaint, which means they are searching for more victims.

3) Know the wide work of the Federal Trade Commission. Visit www.ftc.gov for information.

4) Don't buy from an uninvited door-to-door salesman, telemarketer or e-mail sender.

5) When you have an issue with a company, open a file. Keep a log of the time and date of every call and to whom the call was made. What were you told? What was promised? Ask for the customer service rep's name and employee ID number.

6) Tape these calls, if allowed under your state law. Store them on your computer for later use.

7) Learn how to use small-claims court. Don't hesitate to use this resource to solve your problem.

8) Create your own ID Burn Bag. Collect all your used receipts and other discarded paperwork that discloses personal information such as your Social Security number and store the trash in a bag. Every few months either burn the contents, or better, run it through a paper shredder.

9) Before you sign a contract for any service, know what you are getting and how much you are paying. Ask lots of questions, especially about any promised extras—and make sure everything you agreed upon is written into the final contract. If it's not in writing, it's as if it never happened. GET IT IN WRITING!

10) Obviously, never give your personal information to anyone who pops up and asks for it, either by phone or e-mail. Assume the person is a scammer. Prove otherwise by asking for her phone number and calling her back. Check with the institution she claims to represent to verify.

Most likely, the person and business are NOT legitimate.

11) Don't fall for promises and sales pitches that are too good to be true from e-mails, door-to-door salesmen or telephone solicitors. You haven't won a sweepstakes you never entered. The concrete repair guy offering you a special price doesn't really have any leftover concrete from a neighbor's job. Remember that scammers are con men—short for confidence men—because they are charming, friendly and incredibly slick. They know how to quickly get you to like them and trust them.

12) When you feel wronged by a particular industry, search online for the government agency that regulates the business and file a complaint. Find a national or state association for the industry that may take complaints about its members.

13) Don't pay cash upfront to anybody. If the person insists, tell him to take a hike. First, make him do the job—correctly—and then pay by check or credit card. Get a receipt.

14) Do background checks on companies and individuals on the Internet and with the Better Business Bureau before hiring them.

15) Try to avoid doing business with anyone who advertises in the Yellow Pages who doesn't list a physical street address in the ad. Exceptions can be made for small businesses that don't list an address, but only if you check their references. Ask for a list of their customers. Call the ones at the bottom of the list, not at the top. Ask former customers: "What went wrong? What would you do differently now?"

16) Always check your bills to make sure you aren't overcharged. If you don't know what a charge is, ask.

17) Check return policies at stores before you make a major purchase. Do you get only store credit? Or can you get your money back?

18) If you are a senior, understand that sometimes you might need help. Find "senior advocates" in your community at social service agencies, senior centers or houses of worship who will help you find a solution.

19) When customer service absolutely refuses to solve your problem, threaten to cancel your service. You'll immediately get moved to the front of the line. It's amazing the way that happens.

20) Ask a bunch of questions.

The art of complaining

When it comes to being an artful complainer, I need to heed my own advice offered here. Why? Whenever I call a customer service number for the second or third try to deal with a problem, I find myself getting extremely agitated, threatening and a little abusive. Then I apologize, saying, "I know it's not your fault. It's the person I spoke to before you. He should have fixed this. He said he would, but he didn't. I'm sorry for my frustration."

There is an art to complaining, and I admit to you that I haven't yet mastered it.

My buddy Linda Swindling, a lawyer and negotiations expert, keeps trying to teach me how to get better. Bless her heart! Linda says the key is to create a win-win situation for everyone. She suggests that I treat my nemesis on the phone as a friend and say: "You probably have to answer calls like this all day. Do you have any ideas how we can solve this? What would you do if you were me? Is there anything I'm missing? Tell me, what else do you need from me to make this easier for you?"

While this may be your only complaint, the person on the other end has heard a lot of problems that day.

And remember to be polite. These customer service people are so used to being abused by callers that someone who treats them as a human being is probably someone for whom they want to go the extra mile.

My recommendation is to personalize your situation. Be compassionate and understanding, even though you feel as if you are a victim of a situation they caused.

"I know you didn't cause this problem. Yours is a big company. But it sure would be great if you could help this loyal customer of yours know that I made the right decision by doing business with you."

Or, "You sound like a nice person who wants to help me, and I can't tell you what a change that is. I so appreciate you taking the time to help me!"

Use the person's name: "Molly, you are the best."

Mom always said, "You can attract a lot more flies with honey." So give 'em honey, not heck!

Find your lawmaker and COMPLAIN!

So many problems described in this watchdog call to action are fostered by weak laws that favor your opposition.

Those federal and state laws determine just how much power you have against large corporations, small businesses, utilities and even scammers. Those laws regulate the particular business or industry. They decide who needs a license or certification and what the penalties are. They determine how strong or weak your rights are, too.

Unfortunately, your state and federal lawmakers are more likely to listen to the ones who are screwing you than they are to you. Why? Well, duh. Who gives out the big bucks in the form of campaign contributions? Who has organized political action committees greasing the skids for them, not you?

All you have is the power to complain.

So, as a true member of The Watchdog Nation, when you get into a bad situation that you can't get out of, or when you find a big gaping hole in the law that allows those who you believe are hurting you to prosper, it's imperative that you write, call and e-mail your lawmakers' offices to let them know.

The squeaky wheel gets the grease, right?

How do you find your legislators?

It's easy.

Go to www.votesmart.org and type in your ZIP code. Their names pop up and you click on them. That takes you straight to their contact information.

What are you waiting for? Start squeaking.

File an open-records request

In some situations, you can call on my favorite tool for information—the government open-records request.

In most states, local and state government records (with a few exceptions) are yours. You just have to ask for them. But it's amazing how few citizens use this great tool to get information they need to build their case.

Let's say, for instance, that you get a traffic ticket for running a red light. You don't believe you deserve it. So you do what my friend Rochelle Snow did. She filed an open-records request with her local police department for statistics on how many citations were issued for running a red light. She was trying to find a pattern. She believed the yellow light that she got caught up in was shorter than most yellow lights. Ingenious, but darn, it didn't work. Still, you get the idea.

Research your state open-records law by going to a search engine and typing in: [your state name] and open records law.

Then find a sample letter by typing in: [Your state name] and sample open records request letter.

Here is some advice:

1) Identify your subject. Understand clearly what you want to know and why. Don't ask for every traffic citation ever written. Narrow the scope of your request.

2) Call the government agency—city hall, school district, county government, state agency or other department covered by the state public information act—and ask for the name, title and phone number of the "officer of public records." Call that person and ask how she or he prefers to receive written requests—via e-mail, fax or U.S. mail.

3) In your letter, announce in the first sentence, "This is a request under the state public information act for public records." Mention that you are asking for "access to" and not copies of, at least not yet.

4) I use the following boilerplate language as a catchall: "Any and all information, printed or otherwise, referring to [your subject]. This includes all memos, documentation, e-mails, records,

computerized information and any other information that pertains to this subject." Records are kept in many forms.

5) Next, I write, "In the interest of expediency and to minimize the research and duplication burden on your staff, I would be pleased to personally examine the relevant records if you would grant me immediate access to the requested material." See, you won't actually want every document or record that fits your request. By reviewing all of them, you decide which ones you want to pay for and take with you. Also, write that you are willing to discuss your request further in order to modify it to save time, money and effort. Sometimes, the record keeper will call and explain in what form records are kept and what is available, so that you can narrow the scope of your request.

6) Don't ask the government to compile information for you that doesn't exist, such as requesting a comparison of all traffic citations grouped by the age of those receiving them. It's not their job to create information for you, only to give you what they already have.

7) In most states, it's illegal for a public official to ask why you want the information or what you plan to do with it. If asked, you don't have to tell. Be friendly and professional, not argumentative.

8) Be prepared to pay, but ask for an estimate of costs upfront in your letter. State rules usually allow agencies to charge for staff time and also for duplication costs.

9) When you get the information, you can ask a government official to help you understand it. Although the law usually does not require them to explain it, government officials, especially those who pride themselves on customer service, will help you understand their records. Uh, sorry, I mean your records!

10) Remember that state laws usually allow some information to be exempt from release. But often, the law is written so that it is the government's job to make a case for withholding by appealing to a higher authority, usually the state attorney general.

Open records are a fabulous tool. I include this information here because most non-journalists do not realize how much information is available, just by asking.

Final word: NEVER SURRENDER!

We close with the story of someone I admire, a fellow journalist whose conduct in trying circumstances establishes him as a true member of The Watchdog Nation.

Jeff Prince, a great writer for *Fort Worth Weekly*, fought a jaywalking ticket for eight years. Yes, eight years! For jaywalking!!

Here's what happened:

In 2000, he was waiting for the light to change at a Dallas intersection. Seconds turned into minutes. Two Dallas Area Rapid Transit police officers were standing beside him. He turned to them and said, "Hey, that light's stuck." One of them—Jeff described him as "a sawed-off guy with a military haircut and an attitude"—glared at him but said nothing.

Three or four minutes passed. There was little traffic. All three still stood waiting for the light to change. But it didn't.

The officers turned around and walked up the street.

Jeff then crossed, but as he did so, against the light, he was ordered to stop by a Dallas police officer who rode by on a bicycle. The Dallas officer told him to wait for the DART officers to return.

When they did, sawed-off guy approached, red-faced, and snarled, "So, you wait until we turn our backs and then walk against the light, huh?"

"That light's broken," Jeff protested.

Sawed-off cop wrote him the ticket.

As Jeff later explained, "Try to plead not guilty, and it's hello Alice in Wonderland."

He went to court at lunch hour, only to find out it is closed at the time most people can get away from work to conduct this kind of business.

When the clerk returned, he tried to plead not guilty, but his citation wasn't in the computer. He was told to return in a week. Of course, when he did, his ticket still wasn't there.

"Keep checking back with us," the clerk said.

Like he had time for this.

The clerk told him he could pay the ticket and be done with it.

"Not a chance," Jeff said.

Eventually, he forgot about the ticket.

Five years passed. Then he began receiving collection letters from an annoying law firm hired by DART to collect missing fines. The letters warned, pay $93 or face arrest.

His file was supposedly transferred to another court. He called the court, but the actual file wasn't there. He tried to find out when it would get there but that clerk wasn't helpful either. She refused to answer his questions or tell him her full name.

He received a total of nine letters urging him to pay up—or else.

He contacted the Texas State Commission on Judicial Misconduct, where the executive director told him, "They are just hoping you are going to pay, which means you are pleading guilty and waiving your rights. They are hoping the average citizen will just be scared and pay it."

But Jeff Prince, my man, is no average citizen. He is, after all, a true member of The Watchdog Nation.

Finally, he wrote about it in *Fort Worth Weekly*.

Not long after that, he finally got his day in court. He had a big speech planned. He was ready.

What happened?

Sawed-off guy didn't bother to show.

Ticket dismissed.

A little disappointed after all that, Jeff said, "Dallas County cheated me yet again by not allowing me to face my accuser in court. I'm thinking about appealing my dismissal."

Pretty good, Jeff.

A lesson for us all.

WATCHDOG NATION

One final tip*

*For sticking with me for so long

As a reward for getting this far in the book, here's a Watchdog Nation strategy for finding the name, address, phone number and e-mail address of a high-ranking executive at a big company. This is especially good when the company is driving you crazy.

Call the company's toll-free number and in your sweetest voice say to the person who answers:

"Hello, you know I had the most wonderfully positive experience with your customer call center the other day. Your colleague who helped me was absolutely the best. And I want to write a glowing A-plus letter to the big boss about how great you treat customers like me! Can you give me the contact information of the person who should get this?"

OK, this really is the last tip*

*I like you so much I can't leave

A few of my favorite Web sites:

I get most of my public information on individuals' backgrounds from www.publicdata.com. For $30 a year, I get access to dozens of national and state databases. I trace license plates, find criminal records, hunt down civil lawsuits and dig out a whole lot more. It's worth the investment.

The second site is anywho.com, which lets you do free reverse lookups of a phone number. If you know the phone number, you can find who the phone is listed to and where the person or business is situated. It can't find unlisted numbers, though.

Snopes.com, which differentiates between fact and folklore, is the best place to check e-mails floating around the Web for veracity and also learn the history of many common scams.

Remember that searching BEFORE you buy or hire, rather than afterward, is the smartest thing you can do as a true citizen of Watchdog Nation. You have finished this book, so now you really are one.

SPECIAL THANKS FROM THE AUTHOR

One of my favorite words is epiphany—a sudden insight that changes the way you view the world. Writers like me better have these quite often, or we aren't worth a darn.

Mine came when I realized that 21st-century journalism must be different from the kind I practiced during the early part of my career. Readers don't care what's on my mind. They want a newspaperman like me to work for them, to be on their side, to help them win fights they can't win on their own.

My bosses at the *Star-Telegram* figured this out before I did when they created a new job for me as The Watchdog columnist, which combines column writing, narrative storytelling and investigative reporting. Newspaper ads announced the new position with this tagline: "Finally, you've got somebody in your corner." Now I see that more newspapers need to do this!

From the first day, this column was incredibly popular with readers. The mail is never-ending. The problems never stop. I strive to find solutions, and the best results are shared in this book.

Special thanks to Lois Norder, the editor to whom this book is dedicated. Also thanks to: *Star-Telegram* Executive Editor Jim Witt for believing in me; editor Mark Horvit, now head of Investigative Reporters and Editors; editor Larry Lutz, who helped conceive The Watchdog; book designer Janet Long; artist Ty Walls; copy editors Anita Robeson and Stan Lieber; *Star-Telegram* librarians Marcia Melton, Cathy Belcher, Stacy Garcia and Jodie Sanders; photographers Aaron Dougherty and Norm Sunshine; marketing experts Ed Peters and Homer Plankton; webmaster Kurt Maine, who designed WatchdogNation.com; techno guru Thomas Umstattd Jr.; videographer Chris Gomersall; career coach Alex Ramsey; speaking partner Sally Baskey; indexer Nan Sprester; and motivator Ruth Orren. Thanks also to my family, Karen and the kids, Desiree, Jonathan and Austin, who know Watchdog Man's true identity.

I used to be a columnist. Now, I'm a columnist who helps people.

ABOUT THE AUTHOR

For more than 30 years, Dave Lieber has used his storytelling skills to bring about positive changes. His stories in newspapers and magazines of wrongdoing and right-doing have led to countless changes in governments, schools and communities.

A humorist, storyteller, investigative columnist and public speaker, Dave works as The Watchdog columnist for the *Fort Worth Star-Telegram*.

Co-founder of Summer Santa (www.SummerSanta.org), one of North Texas' largest children's charities, Dave Lieber has structured the non-profit so it's all-volunteer with no paid staff or office. Summer Santa serves several thousand children each year with summer camp scholarships, free medical checkups, summertime toys, back-to-school clothing, school supplies and after-school activities.

For this, he is the winner of the prestigious Will Rogers Humanitarian Award from the National Society of Newspaper Columnists (www.columnists.com). That award is given to the U.S. newspaper columnist "whose work best exemplifies the high ideals of the beloved philosopher-humorist who used his public forum for the benefit of his fellow human beings."

Will Rogers Museums Director Michelle Lefebvre-Carter commented that Dave's work is "a reflection of the Will Rogers humanitarian spirit. Especially today, excellence in newspaper reporting and solid thinking and writing among columnists are vitally important for our democracy."

Be sure to visit Dave's Web site at www.YankeeCowboy.com. The Watchdog Nation Web site and blog can be found at www.WatchdogNation.com.

Here you go….
You earned this…

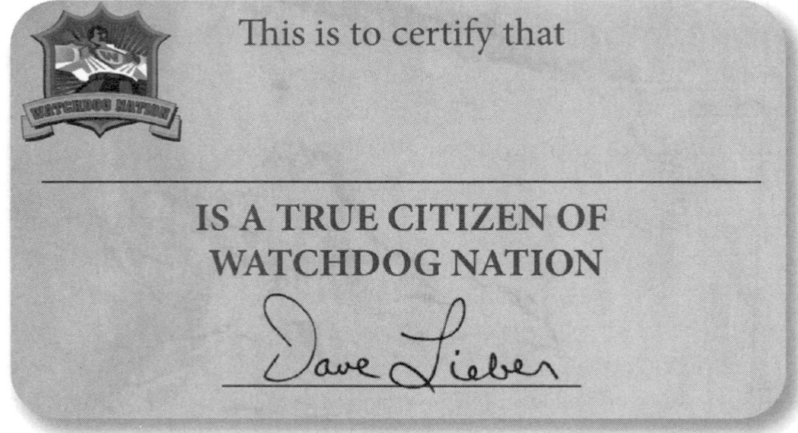

WATCHDOG NATION
This is to certify that
IS A TRUE CITIZEN OF
WATCHDOG NATION
Dave Lieber

If you like this book,
you'll love meeting Dave Lieber

Bring him to your group to speak!

Does your organization want to laugh, learn and get inspired?

Recommend speaker Dave Lieber—and be a hero to your team!

Dave, a member of the National Speakers Association, is one of Texas' most popular speakers.

He'll share how to bite back when businesses and scammers do you wrong. He will empower your group to fight back.

CONTACT: 1-800-557-8166 or dave@yankeecowboy.com

Book and blog site: www.WatchdogNation.com
Dave's site: www.YankeeCowboy.com

Photo by Jeff Claassen

Dave Lieber, the author, takes his job as Watchdog columnist and Leader of The Watchdog Nation seriously—sometimes. For his annual job-performance review at the *Fort Worth Star-Telegram*, Dave wore a Revolutionary War era uniform to meet with his editor, Lois Norder (shown here), to whom this book is dedicated. Reason? Watchdog Nation is revolutionary in every way.

INDEX

A

A-AABLE Overhead Door, 112 -113
AAAble Texas Overhead Door, 112-113
Able Door, 112-113
A&A Insurance Forms Co., 84-85
ABC, 150-151
accuracy of meters, 116-117, 134
Adams, Henry B., 10
adjustable rate mortgage, 72
ADT, 154
advertising scams, 69-71, 79, 146-147
air conditioning, 42, 161
alarm, 154
Alaskan drilling, 69-71
Alice in Wonderland, 170-171
America's Choice Overhead Door Co., 112-113
American Airlines, 69-71, 89
American Petroleum Institute, 132-133
American Stock Exchange, 94-95
American Voyager Travel, 86-87
annoying phone callers, 126-128
annualcreditreport.com, 99
answering machine, 126-128, 135
antibiotics resistant infection, 162-163
apartments, 118-119
appliances, 135, 136-137
API oil recommendations, 132-133
Ask a Bunch of Questions button, 78, 80-82, 164-165
asphalt, 88
associations for reference checking, 118-119, 145
associations to get involved with, 157
AT&T
- annoying phone calls, 126-128, 129
- customer service difficulties, 26-27, 28-29, 30-31, 109, 122-123, 126-128
- phone book delivery problems, 28
- phone card, 120-121
- pitching news media about, 38-39
- prepaid phone card, 120-121
- soldiers' bills from combat zones, 122-123
- U-verse television service, 30-31

attorney general, 18, 35, 67, 87, 94-95, 121, 130, 156, 164-165, 169
auditor, 142-143
auger, 80-82
Austin, Texas, 162-163
automaker, 14-15
automated telephone systems, 96-97, 138-139
automobiles
- offered as prizes, 94-95
- oil changes, 132-133
- towing, 158-159
- work done on, 14-15, 64-65, 154

awards, 11, 94-95
Awards Verification Center, 94-95

B

background check, 19, 21, 79, 135, 164-165, 173
banks
- cashier's check, 146-147
- checking account problems, 140-141, 143-144, 146-147
- data breach, 13
- fake e-mails from, 58-59
- holds on your account, 90-91, 140-141, 146-147
- laws regulating, 143
- manager, 140-141
- teller, 140-141

bankruptcy, 54-56, 69-71
barcodes, 155
Baskey, Sally (speaking partner), 174
bathroom, 80-82
Baxter, Robert (insurance magnate), 148-149
Bean, L.L., 41
beat the price guarantees, 112-113, 138-139
bed, 154-155
Belcher, Cathy, (FWST librarian), 174
Benjamin Franklin Awards, 11
Berra, Yogi, 101
Best Buy, 138-139
Better Business Bureau, 52-57, 62-63, 64-65, 66-67, 69-71, 79, 84-85, 86-87, 94-95, 100-102, 103-105, 112-113, 135, 156, 164-165
bids, 52-57, 64-65, 112-113, 135
bill collector, 36-37
bills, 28, 30-31, 50-51, 55, 76, 106-107, 116-117, 161, 165
blogs, 22-23, 100-102, 136-137, 150-151, 155, 175, 177
BMW, 94-95
book awards, 11
book scam, 24-25
boots by the door, 131
bounced checks, 90-91, 100-102, 103-105, 140-141
bouquet of red roses, 134
box springs, 154
brand names, 136-137
Brown, Edmund G., 67
Bubba's Wholesale, 66
builder, 81, 161
building code, 161
Burgoyne, Ellis, 114-115
button, 78
Buzzmachine.com, 150-151

C

cable television, 76, 125
Calistar, 66-67

cashier's check, 146-147
call centers, 30-31, 32-33, 34, 35, 42-44, 112-113, 122-123, 138-139, 166, 172
Caller ID, 126-128, 130
Call Trace, 126-128
campaign, 156, 157, 162-163, 167
campaign contributions, 167
Canada, 146-147
Capgemeni Energy, 42-44
card of Watchdog Nation, 176
Capital One credit card, 106-107
cars
offered as prizes, 94-95
oil changes, 132-133
towing, 158-159
work done on, 14-15, 64-65, 154
cash payments, 57, 64-65, 94-95, 112-113, 118-119, 146-147, 164-165
cashing in life insurance policies, 148-149
cell phones, 76, 90-91, 122-123
Centers for Disease Control and Prevention, 162-163
certification, 146-147, 167
certified mail, 14, 55, 104, 106-107
certifiers, 142-145
chasing scammers, 135, 173
check fraud, 100-102, 103-105
check processing company, 103-105
check references, 52-57, 66-67, 112-113, 164-165
check verification system, 100-102
checks, 13, 58-59, 66-67, 69-71, 90-91, 100-102, 103-105, 112-113, 146-147
checks offered to you, 58-59, 69-71, 146-147
chutzpah, 134
citation, 168-169, 170-171
citizens group, 157
city government, 116-117, 158-159, 168-169
City University of New York, 150-151
Claassen, Jeff, 178
class action lawsuit, 35, 136-137
cleanup, 80-82
Clinton, William Jefferson, 82
coffee, 72-77
collect calls, 90-91
collecting evidence, 97, 107, 127, 145, 158-159, 161
collection agencies, 13, 36, 39, 100-102, 103-105, 106-107
columnist, 4, 20, 26, 53, 153, 174, 175, 178
columnists.com, 175
Comcast, 150-151
companies
CEO, 49, 89
communications department, 27, 46-48
board of directors, 15, 49
finding executives, 27, 46-48, 103, 150-151, 156, 172
media relations department, 26, 46-47, 104
physical address of, 112-113, 172
searching, 27, 100-102, 142, 150-151, 172
complaining, 14-15, 34, 36-37, 42-44, 46-49, 64-65, 116-117, 122-123, 125, 134, 136-137, 138-139, 140-141, 142-145, 156, 158-159, 164-165, 166, 167
Compass Bank, 140-141, 143-144
computers
using for research, 19, 21, 22-23, 24-25, 46-48, 53-57, 69-71, 72- 77, 79, 84-85, 86-87, 94-95, 108- 110, 118-119, 120-121, 136-137, 138-139, 148-149, 150-151, 158-159
file sharing software, 60-61
protecting, 60-61
troubleshooting, 150-151
concrete, 164-165
confidence men (con men), 164-165
congressman, 143-144
connection fee, 122-123
Consumer Financial Protection Bureau, 107, 144
consumer protection law, 68, 79, 106-107, 156, 157, 161
Consumer Reports, 138-139
consumer rights, 19, 79, 106-107, 136-137, 148-149, 156, 157, 161, 178
Consumers Union, 162-163
Contact Us at Watchdog Nation, 177
contests, 94-95
contracts, 52-57, 64-65, 86-87, 88, 135, 16, 164-165
contractors, 52-57, 135, 161
corporate
CEO, 49, 89
communications department, 27, 46-48
board of directors, 15, 49
finding executives, 27, 46-48, 103, 150-151, 156, 172
media relations department, 26, 46-47, 104
county government, 158-159, 168-169
court, 158-159, 161, 164-165, 170-171
court costs, 161
credit agencies, 29, 39, 96-97, 106-107
credit bureaus, 96-97, 104, 107
credit cards
fake e-mails from, 58-59
interest rate, 76
warranties with, 138-139
credit history, 13
credit references, 37, 39, 96-97, 99
credit report, 13, 96-97, 99
credit card theft, 106-107
credit score, 104
credit union, 104
criminal charges, 52-57
cruises, 94-95
customer forums, 160

customer service call centers, 30-31, 32-33, 34, 35, 42-44, 112-113, 122-123, 138-139, 166, 172
good example of, 41, 89, 125, 138-139, 166
lack of, 14-15, 17-18, 36-39, 41, 42-44, 50-51, 62-63, 114-115, 116-117, 122-123, 125, 134 , 138-139, 140-41, 148-149, 150-151, 160, 164-165, 166
customers
scams, 146-147
treatment of, 40, 41, 42-44, 50-51, 62-63, 89, 114-115, 116-117, 122-123, 125, 134, 138-139, 140-141, 148-149, 150-151, 156, 164-165, 166
customer survey, 18

D

Dallas, 42-44, 84-85, 86-87, 94-95, 112-113, 148-149, 170-171
Dallas Area Rapid Transit, 170-171
Dallas lawyer, 161
Data breach, 13
Davis, Todd
Social Security number of, 96-97
debit card, 90-91
debt collectors, 100-102, 103-105, 106-107
debt dispute, 106-107
Defending the Disadvantaged/First Amendment Award, 11
deposits to bank, 146-147
Deceptive Trade Practices law, 68, 79, 112-113
Dell computer, 150-151
describing your problem, 36-39
Detective Columbo, 48
Detective Dominic LaRocca, 7, 129
digital answering machine, 126-128
Digital Age, 150-151
digital voice recorder, 108-110
direct deposit scams, 58-59
DirecTV, 36-37
Discount Garage Door Co., 112-113
discounts, 42, 76
doctors, 162-163
Dogpile.com, 21, 46
Dominic LaRocca, 7, 129
Do Not Call list, 130
door-to-sale salesmen, 24-25, 88, 164-165
downloads, 60-61
down payment, 56-57
drain, 80-82
driving conditions, 132-133
driveway scam, 164-165
driveway work, 88
drug-resistant bacteria, 162-163
dslreports.com, 160

E

early termination fee, 36-37
eBay, 69-71
electric company
finding executives, 48
meters, 116-117
outsourcing, 42-44
small-claims court, 161
switching, 13
terminating the power, 50-51
waiving reconnection fee, 50
e-mail
AT&T preferred communication, 26
contacting Watchdog Nation, 177
finding addresses, 48, 114-115, 156, 172
fraud, 58-59, 164-165
open record search of, 168-169
overcharges, 122-123
emergency, 90-91
employee ID, 18, 32-33, 34, 35, 42-44, 100-102, 164-165
engine oil change, 132-133
engine sludge, 132-133
Epictetus, 93
Equifax, 96-97, 99, 105
estimated monthly bills, 116-117
estimates in writing, 112-113, 135
evidence, 97, 107, 127, 145, 158-159, 161
excess charges, 161, 164-165
Experian, 96-97, 99, 105
expert witness, 161
extended warranties, 138-139

F

Facebook, 154-155
Fair Credit Reporting Act, 106-107
Fair Debt Collectons Practices Act, 106-107
fake checks, 100-102
fake landlords, 118-119
fake man in the window, 131
FBI, 146-147
FDIC, 144, 146-147
federal Centers for Disease Control and Prevention, 162-163
Federal Communications Commis sion, 120-121
Federal Deposit Insurance Corp., 144, 146-147
federal income tax refund, 58-59, 60-61, 143
federal indictment, 84-85
federal laws, 145, 158-159, 162-163, 167
federal licensor, 142
Federal Reserve Bank, 106-107
Federal Trade Commission, 69-71, 79, 96-97, 99, 100, 103-105, 106-107, 120-121, 146-147,164-165
file a complaint, 42-45, 46-49, 62-63, 116-117, 142-145, 158-159, 161, 164-165

fees, 84-85, 86-87, 106-107, 120-121, 140-141, 143-144, 147-148
file sharing software, 60-61
financial advice, 69-71
financial institutions
  fake e-mails from, 58-59
  holds on your account, 90-91, 140-141, 146-147
finding lawmakers, 167
finding life insurance information, 148-149
fine print, 120-121
FiOs television service, 160
Firefighter Metro Movers, 62-63
First Garage Door, 112-113
Flame Guard and Flame Lock Whirpool water heaters, 136-137
flood (small one), 80-82
flooring, 80-82
flowers, 134
Foley, Jay (ID theft expert), 60-61, 96-97
forged check, 146-147
Fort Worth firefighter, 158-159
Fort Worth Star-Telegram, 20, 53, 174, 175, 178
Fort Worth Water Company, 134
Fort Worth Weekly, 170-171
forums, 160
Frappuccino, 75
fraud alert, 96-97, 99, 104
free gifts, 94-95
free seminars, 88
free trip, 86-87, 94-95

G

garage door repair, 112-113
Garage Door Service, 112-113
Garcia, Stacy, (FWST librarian), 174
Garfield, Bob (media critic), 148-149
gas, 90-91, 132-133
gas meter, 116-117
General Motors, 132-133
getting bids, 53-57, 64-65, 112-113, 135
giveaways, 69-71
Gomersall, Chris (videographer), 174
Google, 21, 22-23, 24-25, 46
Google News Alert, 23
government
  defending consumers, 33, 62-63
  identity theft, 96-97
  investigation, 35
Great Recession, 12, 72
Great Train Wreck of Watauga, 111
Green Berets, 158-159
Green, Scott (computer expert), 60-61

H

hail damage, 52-57
hand-held devices, 24
hardship discount, 76
harassing phone callers, 126-128, 129
health care, 162-163
high-definition technical problems, 160
high-definition TV, 36-37, 138-139
highways, 90-91
Hitchcock, Alfred, 126-128
holds on bank accounts, 90-91, 140-141, 146-147
homebuilder, 161
home renting, 118-119
home-warranty company, 80-82, 141-143
Horvit, Mark (editor), 174
hospital administrators, 162-163
hospital acquired infections, 162-163
hotel, 90-91, 94-95
House Financial Services Committee, 143
house renting, 118-119
houses of worship, 164-165
housing boom, 72
Howard Johnson, 16

I

ic3.gov, 66-67
icemaker, 135
Icerocket.com, 21
income tax refund, 58-59, 60-61, 143
identity theft, 96-97, 99, 100-102, 103-105, 106-107, 164-165
Identity Theft Resource Center, 61, 96-97, 99, 104
infections, 162-163
Infection Reporting System, 162-163
inspections, 80, 158-159, 161
inspectors, 19, 142-145
in-state telephone calls, 120-121
insufficient funds, 140-141
insurance, 52-57, 62, 72-73, 76, 80, 84, 97, 112-113, 148-149, 159
insurance department in state gov ernment, 148-149
Integrity Program, 24-25
interest rate, 76
Internal Revenue Services
  fake e-mails from, 58-59
  tax returns in your computer, 60-61
International Bedding Corporation, 155
Internet
  advertising scams, 69-71, 79
  fraud, 67
  overcharges, 122-123
  phone system, 90-91
  service problems, 160
  using for research, 19, 21, 22-23, 27, 46, 53-57, 64-65, 72-77, 79, 86-87, 94-95, 108-110, 111, 118-119, 120-121, 136-137, 138-139, 148-149, 162-163, 173Internet
  Crime Complaint Center (IC3), 66-67

Inventory control, 155
intra-state telephone calls, 120-121
Investigative Reporters and Editors, 174
investigative reporting, 174
investment opportunities, 69-71, 79, 88
Iraq, 122-123

J

Jarzombek, Jerry (consumer rights lawyer), 106-107
Jarvis, Jeff (blogger), 150-151
jaywalking, 170-171
J. D. Power and Associates, 30
Jefferson, Dr. David (health expert), 162-163
judge, 161, 170-171
judicial misconduct, 170-171

K

Kahak, George (older adult victim), 69-71
keeping records, 32-33, 34, 116-117, 138-139, 148-149, 161, 164-165
Kentucky Central Life, 148-149
Kip, 188
Kolby, 188
Kuwait, 122-123

L

labor, 64-65, 136-137
landlords, 118-119
LaRocca, Dominic, 7, 129
Las Vegas, 86-87, 94-95
lawmakers, 157, 162-163, 167
laws, 68, 79, 96-97, 99, 102, 106-107, 108, 110, 142-145, 157, 158-159, 161, 167-168, 169
lawsuit, 35, 106-107, 136-137, 158-159, 161, 173
lawyer, 79, 86-87, 106-107, 122-123, 161, 166
LCD screens, 138-139
leaks, 80-82, 116-117
legislators, 162-163, 167
liability insurance, 62-63, 112-113
librarian, 21, 68, 111, 118-119, 174
libraries, 54, 111, 118-119, 150-151
licensed, 52-57, 62-63, 118-119, 158-159, 167
licensor, 142-144
Lieber, Dave (author), 11, 89, 155, 174, 175, 176, 177
Lieber, Stan (copy editor), 174
life insurance, 76, 148-149
Lifelock, 96-97, 100-102, 103-105
Lincoln Financial Group, 148-149
Littlefield, Brian, 135
Lloyd, Dr. Jon (superbug expert), 162-163
lobbyists, 157, 162-163, 167
long distance telephone, 31, 90-91
Long, Janet (book designer), 174
loss of records, 96-97
loss protection, 102
lottery, 66-67, 69-71
Lowe's Home Improvement Ware house, 136-137
Lutz, Larry (editor), 174
luxury cars, 94-95

M

Madoff, Bernard, 12
magazine scam, 24-25
mail fraud, 84-85, 146-147
mail problems, 114-115
Maine, Kurt (Webmaster), 174
manager (see supervisor)
man in the window, 131
Marchant, Kenny (U. S. Representa tive), 143-144
Marley, 188
Mason, Perry (lawyer), 161
matrix marketing, 79
MatrixWatch.org, 79
Mattress Giant, 154-155
Maxcy, Lonnie, 134
McGiffert, Lisa (Consumers Union), 162-163
McMurry, Justin, 160
media pitch, 36-39, 46-48
media relations of corporations, 27, 46-48, 104
mediation, 142
medical records, 60-61, 96-97
Melton, Marcia (FWST librarian), 174
membership card, 176
Mercedes, 94-95
meters, 116-117, 134
methicillin-resistant Staphylococcus aureus, 162-163
microphone for digital voice recorder, 108-110
MIB, 148-149
military bills for telephone and data, 122-123
missing life insurance policy, 148-149
missingmoney.org, 148-149
missing property, 148-149
MoneyGram, 146-147
Montgomery Ward, 101
moving company, 62-63, 142
MRSA superbug infection, 162-163
multilevel marketing plans, 79
Mystery Shoppers Providers Associa tion, 146-147
mysteryshop.org, 146-147
mystery shopper scam, 146-147

N

naca.net, 106-107
National Association of Consumer Advocates, 106-107

National Association of Independent Landlords, 118-119
National Best Books Award for Social Change, 11
National Credit Union Administra tion, 144
National Society of Newspaper Columnists, 11, 175
National Speakers Association, 177
Natterer, Jeff (former Green Beret), 158-159
NCO Financial Systems, 106-107
networking marketing, 79
never surrender, 170-171
New Age Marketing Solutions, 69-71
news media, 36-39
newspapers, 36-39, 47, 48, 148-149, 174, 175, 178
newspaper columnist, 4, 20, 26, 53, 153, 174, 175, 178
Next Generation Indie Book Award for Social Change, 11
Nightline, 150-151
non-sufficient funds checks, 140-141
no parking, 158-159
Norder, Lois, 7, 174, 178
North Texas Roofing Contractors, 52-57
notary, 103
nupn.com, 148-149
nurses, 162-163

O

Office of the Comptroller of the Cur rency, 106-107, 142-144
Office of Thrift Supervision, 142-144
oil change, 132-133
owner's manual, 132-133
operator-assisted phone calls, 90-91
open records, 103-105, 145, 158-159, 162-163, 168-169open sores, 162-163
Orlando, 86-87, 94-95
Orren, Ruth (motivator), 174
overcharges, 14, 18, 91, 122-123, 140-141, 158-159, 161, 164-165
overdraft charges, 140-141, 143-144
Overhead AAA Garage Door, 112-113
outsourcing
  electric company, 42-44

P

paper shredder, 164-165
parking, 158-159
parts, 64-65, 68, 135, 136-137, 154-155
patients, 162-163
PayPal, 66-67
pay telephones, 90-91
Pearland, Texas, 100-102
Pennzoil Platinum motor oil, 132-133
permit issuer, 142-144
permits, 52-57
Perry Mason, 161
Peters, Ed (marketing), 174
pharmacy, 90-91
phishing, 58-59
phone calls, 126-128
phone company
  customer service difficulties, 26-27, 28-29, 30-31, 109, 122-123, 126-128
  extra charges on bill, 18, 26
  pitching news media about, 38-39, 46-48
  rates, 76
phone number, 126-128, 164-165
physical street address, 24-25, 118-119, 135, 164-165
pin-striped suit, 161
pipe, 80-82
pitching the media, 36-39, 46-48
plasma TV set, 138-139
Plankton, Homer, 189
plunger, 80-82
plumbing, 80-82, 116-117
police, 25, 67, 100, 104, 109, 126-128, 145, 158-159
policy holders, 148-149
policylocator.com, 148-149
political action committee, 167
pools, 116-117
Porsche, 94-95
post office (See U.S. Postal Service)
post office mail box, 13, 24-25, 84-85, 118-119
Power Sheet, 34
Powerball, 69-71
prepaid phone card, 120-121
pressure point, 142-145
price guarantees, 112-113, 138-139
Prince, Jeff (writer, member of Watchdog Nation), 170-171
privacy, 32-33, 96-97, 99
prizes, 66-67, 69-71, 94-95
product recall, 35
product reviews, 79, 136-137
professional associations, 27, 52-57, 118-119
promises of
  free trips, 86-87, 94-95, 164-165
  job, 69-71, 84-85, 146-147, 164-165
  warranty, 135
property rental, 118-119
prosecutors, 19, 21, 56, 118-119, 145, 158-159
publicdata.com, 22-23, 173
public libraries, 52-57, 111
public pay phones, 90-91
public information act, 168-169
public records, 64-65, 145, 150-151, 158-159, 162-163, 168-169, 173
PVC pipe stuck, 80-82
pyramid scheme, 69-71, 79

Q

Qubein, Nido, 40

R

Ramsey, Alex (career coach), 174
real estate commission, 142
receipts, 118-119, 138-139, 164-165
recession discount, 76
recording telephone calls, 32-33, 34, 35, 42-44, 92, 106-107, 108-110, 126-128, 142, 164-165
records, 60-61, 64-65, 103-105, 116-117, 126-128, 138-139, 145, 148-149, 150-151, 158-159, 161, 164-165, 168-169, 173
red roses, 134
reference checking, 52-57, 64-65, 112-113, 118-119, 135, 168-169, 173
reference librarian, 111, 118-119
refrigerator repair, 135
refund, 18, 33, 58-59, 61, 71, 117, 134, 138, 143, 159
registration with government, 62-63, 118-119, 167
regulators, 142, 145
regulatory agencies, 19, 62-63, 116-117, 142-145, 146-147, 158-159, 164-165, 167, 168-169
Reliable Life Insurance Co., 148-149
renting, 118-119
repairs
  air conditioning, 161
  appliances, 76, 135
  automobile, 14-15, 64-65, 154
  homebuilder, 161
  small-claims court, 161
requesting open records, 103-105, 145, 168-169, 173
resolution seeking, 37, 46-49, 142-145, 158-159, 161
restaurants, 90-91
return policies, 164-165
reverse psychology, 92
reverse telephone lookup, 173
reviews, 79, 136-137
Rio Grande National Life Insurance Co., 148-149
rip-offs, 21, 22-23, 79
roaming charges, 122-123
Robeson, Anita (copy editor), 174
roofers, 52-57
roses, 134
Rotary Club, 46
Royal Purple motor oil, 132-133

S

Sacramento, California, 67
sales, 22-23, 66-67, 79, 86-87, 94-95, 110, 112-113, 120-121, 122-123, 132-133, 138-139, 146-147, 156, 164-165
Samsung, 138-139
Sanders, Jodie, (FWST librarian), 174
Santa Claus, 66
satellite TV, 36-37
scams
  Great Era of, 18, 69-71, 79, 164-165
  protecting against, 21, 24-25, 69-71, 79, 108-111, 112-113, 118-119, 164-165, 173
school districts, 168-169
search engines
  Dogpile.com, 21, 46
  Google.com, 21, 23, 24-25, 46
  Icerocket.com, 21
  using them, 19, 21, 22-23, 24-24, 64-65, 79, 84-85, 86-87, 94-95, 108-110, 118-119, 120 -121, 136-137, 138-139, 142-145, 148-149, 160, 162-163, 173
  viewzi.com, 173
security alarm, 154
security freeze, 99, 103-105
Securities and Exchange Commis sion, 106-107
senior citizens
  advocates, 164-165
  falling prey to scams, 69-71
  life insurance, 148-149
  services for, 69-71, 164-165
senior discount, 76
Shaw Tatum Roofing, 52-57
sheriff's department, 66-67, 103-105, 118-119
shredder, 164-165
sludge, 132-133
small-claims court, 158-159, 161, 164-165
snopes.com, 173
social media, 153-155
Social Security number, 32-33, 58-59, 60-61, 96-97, 164-165
Society of Professional Journalists, 11
soldiers' telephone and data bills, 122-123
speaker, 177
special forces, 158-159
speeches, 177
Sprester, Nan (indexer), 174
sprinkler company, 116-117
Stanford, R. Allen, 12
star witness, 161
Starbucks, 72-77
state agencies, 62-63, 90-91, 116-117, 142-145, 148-149, 158-159, 168-169
state attorney general, 18, 35, 67, 87, 94-95, 121, 130, 156, 164-165, 169
state banking department, 140-141, 144
state insurance department, 148-149
state law, 68, 79, 94-95, 156, 157, 158-159, 162-163, 164-165, 167, 168-169
state real estate commission, 142
state trooper, 101
stock, 69-71
StopHospitalInfections.org, 162-163
state licensor, 142-144
strategy of The Watchdog Nation, 142-145, 158-159, 172
Stream Energy, 50-51

sue, 106-107, 145, 158-159,161
superbug infection, 162-163
Superior Garage Door, 112-113
supervisor
complaining to, 14-15, 36-37, 43, 46-49, 64-65, 122-123, 125, 140-141, 156
surrender, 170-171
sweepstakes, 164-165
swimming pools, 116-117
Swindling, Linda (negotiation expert), 166
synthetic oil, 132-133
synthesized checks, 100-102

T

taping calls, 17-18, 32-33, 34, 35, 42-44, 92, 106-107, 108-110, 126-128, 142, 164-165
Tarrant County Public Health, 162-163
Tatum Contracting, 52-57
tax refunds, 58-59, 60-61, 143
tax returns, 58-59, 60-61
TeleCheck, 100-102, 103-105
telemarketer, 164-165
telephone calls
annoying, 126-128, 129
recording, 32-33, 34, 35, 42-44, 92, 106-107, 108-110, 126-128, 142, 164-165
telephone call centers, 30-31, 32-33, 34, 35, 42-44, 112-113, 122-123, 138-139, 166, 172
telephone company
automated phone systems, 96-97, 138-139
customer service difficulties, 26-27, 28-29, 30-31, 90-91, 122-123, 126-128
finding executives, 48
private number, 126-128, 129, 164-165, 173
service problems, 160
telephone books, 28, 112-113, 173
telephone number of Watchdog Nation, 177
television, 30-31, 36-37, 138-139, 160
telecommunications, 42-44, 90-91, 122-123, 126-128, 148-149
terminating electricity, 50-51
termination fee, 37
testimony, 161
testing meters, 116-117, 134
thermocouple, 136-137
thumbprint, 105
ticket from police, 110, 168-169, 170-171
Time magazine, 148
timeshares, 94-95
Time Warner Cable, 125
toasters, 140-141
toilet, 80-82
Tooth Fairy, 66
towing companies, 158-159
tracing phone calls, 126-128, 129
traffic light, 170-171
traffic tickets, 110, 168-169, 170-171
Transmission, 64-65
transportation law, 158-159
TransUnion, 96-97, 99, 105
travel agent, 86-87
travel club
frustration with, 16, 17, 86-87
seminar, 88
travel ID, 86-87
Travelers Advantage Club, 16
tricks, 92, 129-131, 134, 166
TRS Recovery, 100-102, 103-105
Turner, Wes (publisher), 174
TV, 30-31, 36-37, 138-139, 160
TV news, 36-39
Twilight Zone, 40, 126-128
Twitter, 23, 153-155
TXU Electric
outsourcing, 42-44

U

Umstattd, Jr., Thomas (techno guru), 174
unclaimed property, 148-149
unclaimed.org, 148-149
Underwood, Gary (Time Warner Cable), 125
United Republic Bank of Omaha, 146-147
USA Book News, 11
USA Today, 78
U.S. Congress, 90-91
U.S. Postal Inspectors, 84-85, 146-147
U.S. Postal Service, 84-85, 114-115, 147
U. S. Treasury, 143
utilities (see by specific type)
U-verse television service, 30-31

V

vacation homes, 118-119
Verizon, 160
viewzi.com, 173
voice message system, 138-139
volunteering, 157, 160
votesmart.org, 167

W

Wal-Mart, 13, 100-102, 103-105
Wall, Ty (book artist), 174
warranty, 135, 138-139
washing hands, 162-163
Watchdog Nation
buttons of, 78
column, 175
contact information, 177
determination of the, 116-117
e-mail to, 177, 186

house detective, 129
learning to become a member, 80-82
Manifesto, 9
membership card, 176
playing for keeps, 109
principles of, 22-23, 32-33, 35, 72-77, 142-145, 164-165
purpose of, 18-20
revolution by consumers, 150-151, 178
speaker, 177, 186
speeches, 177, 186
strategy advice, 34, 158-159, 142-145
surrender, never, 170-171
telephone number of, 177
Web site, WatchdogNation.com, 12, 155, 177, 186
WatchdogNation.com, 12, 155, 177, 186
water, 80-82, 116-117, 134
water company, 116-117, 134
water company meters, 116-117, 134
water heater, 136-137
waterheatersettlement.com, 136 -137
Watauga, Texas, 111
Western Union, 146-147
Whirlpool, 136-137
Will Rogers Humanitarian Award, 175
wiretapping, 108-110
Witt, Jim (editor), 174
witnesses, 161
word-of-mouth advertising, 40
World Wide Web
using for research, 19, 21, 22-23, 27, 46, 53-57, 72-77, 84-85, 86-87, 94-95, 108-110, 118-119, 120-121, 136-137, 138-139, 148-149, 162-163, 173
work-at-home jobs, 69-71, 84-85
wounds, 162-163
written bids and estimates, 52-57, 64-65, 112-113, 135, 164-165

X

Y

Yahoo, 69-71
Yankee Cowboy, 175, 186
YankeeCowboy.com, 175, 186
Yellow Pages, 112-113, 164-165
YMMSS (Your Money Machine Suc cess System), 79
youtube.com, 23, 150-151, 155, 156

Z

zoominfo.com, 27, 46, 48

DAVE LIEBER'S

WATCHDOG NATION

MY NOTES

DAVE LIEBER'S
WATCHDOG NATION
MY NOTES

DAVE LIEBER'S
WATCHDOG NATION
MY NOTES

DAVE LIEBER'S

WATCHDOG NATION

MY NOTES

Ladies and gentlemen, Watchdog Man has left the building.

Book site: www.WatchdogNation.com

Dave Lieber's site: www.YankeeCowboy.com